GOD

dialogue of faith

GOD

AN HONEST CONVERSATION
FOR THE UNDECIDED

by E. GLENN WAGNER

WATERBROOK
PRESS

GOD
PUBLISHED BY WATERBROOK PRESS
2375 Telstar Drive, Suite 160
Colorado Springs, Colorado 80920
A division of Random House, Inc.

All Scripture quotations, unless otherwise indicated, are taken from the *Holy Bible, New International Version*®. NIV®. Copyright © 1973, 1978, 1984 by International Bible Society. Used by permission of Zondervan Publishing House. All rights reserved. Scripture quotations marked (MSG) are taken from *The Message*. Copyright © 1993, 1994, 1995, 1996, 2000, 2001, 2002. Used by permission of NavPress Publishing Group. Scripture quotations marked (NLT) are taken from the *Holy Bible, New Living Translation,* copyright © 1996. Used by permission of Tyndale House Publishers, Inc., Wheaton, Illinois 60189. All rights reserved. Scripture quotations marked (KJV) are taken from the *King James Version*.

Italics in Scripture quotations reflect the author's added emphasis.

The author has made every effort to ensure the truthfulness of the stories and anecdotes in this book. In a few instances, names and identifying details have been changed to protect the privacy of the persons involved.

ISBN 1-57856-783-1

Copyright © 2005 by E. Glenn Wagner

Published in association with the literary agency of Alive Communications, Inc., 7680 Goddard Street, Suite 200, Colorado Springs, Colorado 80920.

Library of Congress Cataloging-in-Publication Data
Wagner, E. Glenn, 1953–
God : an honest conversation for the undecided / E. Glenn Wagner.—1st ed.
    p. cm. (Dialogue of Faith)
  Includes biographical references.
  ISBN 1-57856-783-1
  1. God. I. Title. II. Series
BT103.W34 2004
231—dc22   2004018610

Printed in the United States of America
2005—First Edition

10 9 8 7 6 5 4 3 2

To honest pursuers of truth

CONTENTS

PART 3: A CLEARER LOOK AT GOD

ACKNOWLEDGMENTS

WaterBrook Press and Ron Lee—for catching the vision for this project.

John Fanella—for his friendship and help in bringing this book to reality.

Doug Banister and Bryan Loritts—for being a part of the launch of the Dialogue of Faith series.

Chip MacGregor—for getting the idea out there.

Bev Modzell—for administrating the details of ministry.

And Susan—for being such an encouragement and support in our journey of life together.

THE GOD QUESTION

L et me tell you about someone my friend John recently met. Jenna showed up one day at his church wanting to talk to someone about spiritual things. John was the pastor on call, so he went to the lobby to meet her.

After introducing themselves, John and Jenna exchanged small talk for a few minutes. John suspected that something bigger was coming, but Jenna apparently needed time to work up to it. Then the conversation turned more serious.

"My mom died about two years ago," Jenna began. "She was everything to me." It was clear that Jenna was hurting.

"Some friends gave me a Bible," she continued. "I've been trying to read it, but I just don't get it. I tried to read it like a novel, but it just isn't working."

"Well, the Bible doesn't read like a novel," John explained. "By the time you get to the book of Leviticus in the Bible, it's no longer a page-turner. So instead of talking about the Bible, why don't we start by talking about God? Tell me what you believe about God and the afterlife."

"Well," Jenna said, "both of my parents were Jewish."

"So you're Jewish?" John asked.

"I guess so," she said. "But I haven't gone to synagogue in years."

"I'm guessing, then, that you don't believe that Jesus is God," John said.

"Why do you say that?" Jenna replied.

"Well, because Jews don't believe that Jesus is the Son of God. They believe monotheism makes such a thing impossible. Also, Judaism traditionally teaches that the Messiah hasn't come yet."

"I didn't know that," she said.

THE QUESTION OF RELIGION

Since Jenna's parents were Jewish, John assumed that she was familiar with some of the teachings that differentiated Judaism from Christianity. But as their conversation indicated, Jenna had little to no understanding of religion, even the religion of her parents. In that sense, she's very typical. Jenna was Jewish by birth, but in terms of a religious belief system, she was not Jewish or Christian or anything else. Perhaps she is best described as spiritually open.

As Jenna and John talked further, Jenna explained that her mom was her god, and now, with her mother gone, Jenna was searching for a place to belong or something that would help her make sense of her tremendous loss. "I have to believe she is still with me. Maybe it's like that *Other Side* show; maybe she can hear me when I talk to her. I believe she can. That's about the only thing I believe."

"So you believe there is something more than what you see, that there is a spiritual world?" John asked.

"Yes, there's more than what we see," Jenna said. "But if God wanted us to know he's there, why didn't he make it more obvious? Why didn't he give us proof? Do I just have to take a blind leap of faith? And this Jesus I read about; he really confuses me. He just keeps saying the same thing over and over, and the points he makes don't make any sense at all."

"Let's take a walk," John suggested. "Sometimes it's easier to talk when walking." What John learned about Jenna next helped him understand what she was feeling.

Jenna said, "I had such a close relationship with my mom. I could tell her anything, and I felt safe with her. I could be myself, and I never doubted that she loved me. Why don't I feel this way with God? I feel like he doesn't want me to know him like that."

"Okay," John said. "What else?"

"I also can't deal with the idea that God loves everyone. I mean, I've made my mistakes and all. I was in the navy, and I'll admit I lived the sailor life. But I'm not a bad person. I don't want to be sitting in heaven with my mom and have Charles Manson or Jeffrey Dahmer come walking up to me. I don't care if they found God or not; they don't deserve to be in the same place as me and my mom."

"Do you feel any guilt about your life?" John asked.

"No," she said. "I don't think sex before marriage is wrong. Sometimes my mom made me feel guilty about it, but I don't have any guilt when it comes to God."

"So you don't feel like you need forgiveness?" John asked.

"No, not really," she replied. "I just want to know what's true. I just want to make sense out of all this."

"Are you dissatisfied with your life?" John asked, trying to identify some tangible need in Jenna's life.

"No, I'm actually pretty happy. I've got friends. I've got a good job. Haven't met Mr. Right yet, but I'm okay with that."

John tried his best to explain to Jenna that God is real and that he wants to have a relationship with her. He told her that God has revealed himself to humanity and that he hasn't left us to wonder what he's like. John tried to explain that God is the one who could fill the void in Jenna's life, although he realized that she didn't perceive having any huge needs, other than missing her mom terribly. John encouraged her to keep seeking—another term she didn't understand. He suggested that they talk again sometime, so they exchanged phone numbers.

TALK ABOUT GOD

I was intrigued with John's conversation with Jenna. There were no secret formulas, no guaranteed steps to success, no brilliant insights that changed her life. Just an honest conversation about one person's interest in God. In other words, this was a normal conversation. And it's in honest conversations that most of us discover God.

Jenna's comments reflect a common view of people today: God is no longer necessary. He may be interesting or possibly even enigmatic, but not much more than that.

In my work as a pastor, at times I felt more like a tour guide than a spiritual director. I would point out the sights to interested passersby, who were just tourists with little long-term interest in God. They had heard about God from someone else, a parent or grandparent perhaps. So they figured they'd come and check out the sights.

But it's hard to convince tourists to stay since there are always so many other things to look at—so much more in life to experience.

Frank Schaeffer, son of theologian-philosopher Francis Schaeffer, uses two metaphors to describe how a lot of people view God. The first is a dinosaur metaphor. God is to the postmodern era what dinosaurs are to the modern era. We think God used to live here. We see evidence of human encounters with him. We have found the remains of a whole civilization that lived alongside him, or at least aware of him. But we don't see him any longer. He left behind some fossils that give us clues to his former existence, but no one expects him to walk the earth again.

Friedrich Nietzsche said, "Where is God gone?... I mean to tell you! We have killed him—you and I! We are all his murderers!... Do we not hear the noise of the grave-diggers who are burying God?... God is dead! God remains dead!"[1] What he really meant was, "God is extinct."

Some people like to imagine what God was like, the way we imagine what a T. rex was like. We've built museums (called churches) that give hints of prehistoric days when the dinosaur roamed the earth. We've built research centers (called seminaries) that study the prehistoric creature. It's all somewhat interesting, but for many it's nothing more than a detached, impersonal examination of history. It's hardly exciting to look at dust-covered remains and reconstructions of God within glass enclosures.

But how do we explain the random reports and purported evidence that God is doing things on earth—not in a long-ago era, but today? I've noticed a *Jurassic Park* scenario in many people's lives. For years we've thought the dinosaur named God was extinct. But then someone encounters him. Perhaps even a firm adherent of the dinosaur theory encounters him. We begin to wonder if the dinosaur isn't extinct after all.

Schaeffer's second metaphor is that of a nursing home. If we don't believe God is extinct, we assume that he's been warehoused in the Alzheimer's wing of a nursing home. He has lost touch with reality. He needs constant care just to keep breathing and to remain even remotely in touch with our changing times.

Many of us still feel obligated to drop by every now and then to pay our respects. We listen to him mumble and grumble, but none of it makes much sense. Can't someone just put him out of his misery? It seems so cruel to keep him alive in a world that is no longer recognizable to him. It seems like a waste of time and effort to keep him around, but we suppose it's the right thing to do. We don't rely on him for anything, but somehow we just can't find it within ourselves to pull the plug.[2]

A FAITH MAP

Maybe one of those metaphors touches on your view of God. He's extinct and long gone, or he's around but out of touch and ineffective. Or perhaps that describes your former view, but now you find yourself confronting the real God who somehow checked out of the nursing home or has chosen to once again walk the planet. He's active. He has friends. And he has a lot to say to the rest of us.

With so many people today discovering or rediscovering God, I've written this book as a faith map to help you locate yourself in relation to God.[3] Finding your way through the maze of faith can feel perilous. I'm traveling this journey just like you are, so I don't have all the answers. But I'm glad to share with you where I've been and what I've seen along the way.

Maybe we'll even find God.

part one

TRADING ANSWERS
FOR QUESTIONS

*Facts About God Don't Quench
Our Soul's Thirst*

SQUARING OFF WITH GOD

Raising Questions About Answers

Reading a book was once thought to be a one-sided process, but it's really not. While it's true that the author has the microphone, the reader isn't just passively sitting in the audience, accepting everything the author presents. The reader is asking questions, challenging the author's assumptions, weighing the author's assertions and arguments. In that sense, this book is a dialogue, a conversation between you and me.

Now let me tell you a bit about myself. I'm Glenn Wagner. I live in Charlotte, North Carolina, but grew up outside Philadelphia. I'm married and have two kids who are grown and living on their own. I ride a Harley. (I just sold my Dyna Wide Glide and got the hundredth anniversary Road King Classic.) My wife, Susan, and I just moved into a different home, so right now we're in that wonderful, frustrating stage of unpacking boxes and trying to remember where we put everything. Our dog (actually my wife's dog) is trying to adapt to her new domain. The cat hasn't been seen for several days, and I'm undecided about whether I'm going to give our new address to some of the relatives.

On the career side, I'm founder and president of FutureLead, an organization committed to equipping people to live and lead with purpose and passion. Prior to this I served as senior pastor of Calvary Church, a Christian faith community located in Charlotte, North Carolina. I also served as vice president and minister at large of Promise Keepers, an organization that helps men become positive influencers in their homes.

I've spent much of my adult life pursuing higher education. In the process I've earned a couple of doctorates and written a number of books. I don't say that to brag, since education is how we discover how much we don't know. I mention it just to give you a feel for my personality. I'm sort of an introvert. Although I love people and have devoted my life to serving people, I really enjoy being alone. I like to explore ideas. At social functions Susan connects with everybody in the room. I prefer to get to know one or two people really well and find out what they think about stuff.

How About You?

So why did you pick up this book? Why are you interested in reading about God? Whatever the reason, it's fine with me. The violence and injustice and brutality of life that we see presented on the nightly news are moving a lot of people to explore the topics of God and faith. Maybe you're merely curious, or you're angry, or you're skeptical. You might be disappointed, feeling burned by God. Or ignored by God. Or perhaps you just feel like looking around, seeking something bigger than the life you're most familiar with. I understand, because I've been there too.

When I was growing up, my brothers and I were forced to go to church twice a week. But even with all that exposure to people who believed in God and all the talk about God, it never made sense. Somehow the God/church thing just didn't connect with me. It wasn't until I was twenty and facing some personal challenges that someone helped me understand some of the deeper needs and longings in my life—things I sensed were there but hadn't examined very closely. In the years since then, I've experienced times when I've struggled and questioned and wrestled with God.

It's great when people don't have everything figured out, because that's where I am. My exploration of God has been a combination of enthrallment and disaster. On the good side, I've experienced God in some amazing ways. For example, I saw God heal a friend who had been given only months to live. I've also experienced God—or should I say, failed to experience God—in the teeth of some pretty tough pain. I've sat at the bedside of a friend and watched her die, while God appeared to be occupied elsewhere, taking care of something else—but not my friend.

If you're looking for someone to tell you that God takes away all the hurt in life, you've come to the wrong place. If you're looking for someone who has it all figured out and is ready to bless the world with his wisdom, it's time to find another book to read. The difference God has made in my life is that he has provided a divine perspective that helps me deal with both pain and pleasure. And he has given me the grace and peace to endure both extremes.

So let's talk.

Imagine that you and I meet as total strangers in a coffee shop. I've met some really intriguing people this way. They come from all walks of life and from all kinds of faith backgrounds. We run into each other at Starbucks and chat as we sip our venti no-fat lattes. I love hearing what's on people's minds.

What's your story? How have you gotten to where you are today? What has been the most painful thing in your life up to now? What has brought you the most pleasure? If you could understand one thing about God, what would it be? Take some time to write your answers to these questions in a separate journal.

The best place to start thinking and talking about God is where you're at right now. In fact, that's the *only* place we can start. It does no good to imagine that life is smoother or more rewarding than it really is. Some people think you've got to have your act together before you can talk about God, because otherwise he won't come around. I've discovered that it's just the opposite. God is incredibly interested in those of us who have the biggest disappointments, the most troubling questions, the deepest regrets over the worst mistakes.

I've seen evidence of God all over the world, and I suspect you've seen some signs of divine life yourself. I've seen God do some amazing things in people's lives, and it makes for a great conversation. I promise not to force anything on you. Let's just talk.

Squaring Off with God

You've probably heard preachers or friends or relatives act as if they've got all the answers when it comes to God. Somehow, a lot of people think the best way to talk about God is to answer questions about him—as if that can really be done.

That's not an approach I recommend, because it doesn't leave room for honest wrestling. A better way to talk about God is to be free to question, challenge, argue, and live with tension. I won't try to nail down every topic in a once-for-all solution. I'm still wrestling with many of these issues myself.

If I've learned anything, it's that when it comes to God, there is always struggle and tension. We struggle with paradoxes like:

- God is loving, but he permits war.
- God is good, yet evil exists.
- God is distant, yet he is all around us.
- God knows everything, but he declines to tell me what's going to happen next.
- God can do anything, yet most of the human population has to struggle just to survive.
- God is real, but he remains invisible.
- God is God, but he became a man.

I've heard all the pat answers, but none of them satisfies my biggest questions. There are many things about God we'll always wrestle with, and considering that God is infinite, I'm willing to accept this. My relationship to God is not dependent on having all of my questions answered; rather, it's dependent on knowing and believing that *God is the answer*. Even when I don't understand what's happening, I'm comfortable knowing God does.

Relating to God looks a lot like what happens in the movies *The Matrix* and *Field of Dreams*. You only get insight and direction for taking the next step, not a map for the entire journey. The challenge is to keep following God's voice even though you don't have all the information. In the Bible, God asked Noah to build a giant boat to save his family from the rains that would pour from the sky and flood the earth. Noah had never seen such a flood before. He lived in a dry, landlocked region where it would have been inconceivable to have enough water to float this gigantic craft. Talk about living with tension. Talk about not having it all figured out ahead of time.

You and I need to be prepared for a similar experience—hearing from God without having all the information we'd like to have.

MORE QUESTIONS THAN ANSWERS

If you come away from our conversation feeling that you've got God all figured out, something will have gone terribly wrong. God *can't* be completely figured out. The idea that we can somehow quantify God if we just study him enough was a mistaken goal of Enlightenment rationalism. It just doesn't work—but I probably don't need to tell you that.

Many aspects of God simply don't make sense to the finite mind. It doesn't matter how long or how thoroughly you study God, you will always come away with some unanswered questions, some seeming paradox, some mystery. Yet this is what makes God, well, God. He isn't a lab rat that we can keep in a cage and do experiments on. He's a mysterious Being who transcends our best attempts to figure him out.

For example, God is a transcendent Being who is also right here with us. He's an infinite and eternal Being who also reveals himself in the space-time continuum. He's a just and holy God who figured out a way to restore our relationship with him, even in our broken condition.

I'd like to share with you some of what I've discovered on my journey with God, and I hope you'll write down some of your experiences. Here's the deal: I believe every one of us has some sense that there is more in the universe than what we can experience with our five physical senses. I think we all have a feeling that somewhere there is a higher Being who has something to do with life on this planet. We may express this sense in different ways, but I believe it's our thirst for God, a deep inner longing to know him, that leads to questions and investigations and journeys of exploration to try to find him.

None of us is looking for dry facts. We don't want logical proof that the idea of God is a perfectly reasonable assumption. Who cares? It's not facts about God that quench our soul's thirst; it's God himself.

This is where I am in my journey toward God—pursuing him, chasing him, trying to catch fresh glimpses of him. Each day presents new opportunities to do this, and I've come to believe that my pursuit will never end. At least, I hope it never ends.

part two

FINDING GOD ON THE HORIZON

Why Are Most People's Ideas About God So Narrow and Confining?

TRADING BOXES
FOR HORIZONS

Gaining a Bigger View of God

Most of what I've heard people say about God is a view from inside a box. People tend to make claims about God from within narrow, predetermined parameters. This has always been a problem for me because God can't be contained within human parameters. Any attempt to stuff God into a box, keeping him in there until we decide to let him out, is futile at best and blasphemous at worst.

Don't misunderstand me. God makes himself knowable. And humans can understand some of the parameters within which God has chosen to reveal himself. In fact, the few things God has told us about himself are enough to keep us occupied for the rest of our lives. Because he is transcendent (beyond the here and now), he is always greater than we can imagine and beyond our ability to fully understand. But if you want to know who God is and what he's like, you can find out. God is not a riddle we can never hope to solve. He's more like a diamond waiting to be discovered.

HEY JACK, GET IN THE BOX

Have you ever been beaten up by someone who is trying to force you into his or her box? I have. When I was with an organization called Promise Keepers, which tried to pull together large numbers of men who held a variety of religious views, I constantly caught grief because we weren't narrow enough. Some of the critics didn't want Catholics hanging around with Protestants. Others didn't want Protestants who were big into the presence and activity of the Holy Spirit to be included. Still others chose not to participate because they didn't really want anyone to be there but themselves. Talk about narrow.

One guy said, "Unity is great, so long as the people we're united with are true Christians." My question is, By whose standard? Usually a person who says such things really means "a true Christian according to *my* definition." People think they have the right to judge what's right for everyone else. And people usually want to judge other people on secondary matters. Instead of seeking agreement on, say, matters that relate to the nature of God, they want to key in on issues such as church traditions or styles of music. People get picky about how you pray or the terminology you use. It's amazing what issues some people try to cram into boxes. It's as though the box is the important thing, not the God we're trying to get in touch with.

Many people within the church (the word we use to describe all of the Christian believers throughout the world) are pretty hung up on their boxes. And, like people in any area of discourse, they can be wrong. They can be hurtful. They can be odd. They can be overly zealous. They can be angry and arrogant. They can also be boring, irrelevant, and apathetic. My hope is that Christians will learn to be more loving and more concerned about maintaining relationships than with safeguarding their petty preferences.

MY, IT'S DARK IN HERE

The problem begins with boxes. And the truth is, everyone, regardless of whether or not they're religious, has the tendency to build boxes. But you can't talk about God from inside a box—any box. Boxes are dark, confining, and exclusive. You're either in or you're out; you're never in process, never moving toward something or away from anything. But for some reason, most of the talk about God occurs from inside an ugly cube of man-made cardboard. And those inside the box issue dire warnings to anyone who might try to shake the box or, God forbid, try to open the lid to let some light inside.

Boxes do the exact opposite of what God does:

- They hold things together, keeping everything in place. But God wants to shake us up.
- They group similar things together, but God prizes diversity and dissimilarity. He wants to mix in some variety.
- They keep things out, protecting what's inside from being "tainted." But God wants to bring new things into our lives.
- They are barriers, separating those who "belong" from those who don't. But God wants to break down walls between people.
- They are closed off and taped shut, trapping stale air inside and sealing out the breeze. But God wants us to be free. He wants to breathe new life into us every day.

Let's begin differently, by flattening the boxes. There are religious boxes that restrict a person's view of God to whatever his or her religious upbringing has taught. There are ethnic and cultural boxes that assume God conforms to certain cultural biases[1] or that God really does prefer certain ethnic groups over others. There are academic boxes that keep God at arm's length, causing people to study him dispassionately as if he's the thesis for a research paper. On the other hand, there are experiential boxes that discard the use of reason in favor of pure experience—as if God is only what you feel him to be.

Then there are the individualistic boxes that limit our thoughts about God to what he can do for *me*. And the sentimental boxes that associate God only with Easter dinner at Grandma's or beautiful music played at a wedding. And I know you've run into the political boxes that try to convince people that God always votes straight-ticket Republican or Democrat or Green Party or Libertarian or Progressive—depending on who you're talking to. There are nationalistic boxes, where people sing "God Bless America" but never even hum quietly "God Bless Iraq." And of course, there's the mystical box, which assumes that God is present only when weird things are going on. (If it doesn't make the hair stand up on the back of your neck, then God's hanging out somewhere else.) Or if you prefer, there's the naturalistic box, where all those so-called weird things have a perfectly rational explanation.

There are people who hop from one box to another, depending on which view is most popular at the time. Like dieters who dump Atkins to follow the South Beach craze. Others keep several boxes handy, jumping in and out of them depending on their mood or who they're with at the moment. This gives the illusion of being open-minded, but it's really just moving from one prison cell to another.

Even atheism and agnosticism and skepticism are boxes. Either God isn't out there, or maybe he's out there, but even if he is, we have no way of knowing for sure. These boxes keep people safely inside where they'll be in no danger of tripping over God by accident.

When you're looking for God, you can get worn out by all the box talk. So let's forget the boxes and talk about God instead. By climbing out of our respective boxes, we can enjoy dialogue. And maybe we'll even encounter God—on his terms rather than ours.

A far more satisfying way to pursue God is to look around us and recognize his work and presence. I don't need a new box that purports to explain him better than the old box did. I just need to learn to see him right where I live.

I see God's power in people like Ted and Amy, who moved from Canada to the same neighborhood where Ed and Carol live. Amy and Ted grew up with a knowledge of God but didn't feel connected to him. Ed and Carol began to point them to the God who wants to have a relationship with them. Ted and Amy recognized their need and desire for God and entered into a relationship with him. They now tell others how their new relationship with God has reignited their lives. They have moved from religion to relationship. They are not the same people they used to be.

This is one of the places I've learned to look for God. He shows up in the lives of real people who have had real encounters with him.

GOD ON THE HORIZON

No matter how big or sturdy a box is, it's still a box, with all the limitations of a box. The notion of a box-based epistemology (way of knowing) is faulty from the outset. If we've learned anything in our pursuit of knowledge, it's that we must first understand the bigger picture before we can grasp the details. In literary criticism, for example, we would never take an isolated passage and interpret the entire work based on that one passage. In the medical field, most doctors wouldn't assess your health without first learning about your family's health history. In photography, some images can only be seen in context using a wide-angle lens. To really understand something, we must think holistically, not compartmentally.

That is perhaps the best reason to kick aside the boxes and start talking about God in the context of life, the world, and even the universe. Instead of gazing into the confines of our boxes, let's study the horizon.

One of my friends told about a trip he and his wife made to Switzerland. Arriving in Frankfurt, Germany, at sunset, they decided to go ahead and drive to their destination. The beauty of Switzerland was veiled by the thick darkness, but they arrived safely and checked into their hotel. Early in the morning they awoke to the sound of cowbells clanging and sunlight pouring into their open window. They looked outside to find that they were overlooking one of the most spectacular views on the face on the earth. Perched high in the Swiss Alps, they beheld swooping valleys and brilliant vistas—the most breathtaking view imaginable. But they didn't know all of this beauty was out there until sunrise, when they looked out at the horizon.

This is the way it is with God. As long as we choose not to look beyond the walls that surround us, we'll never encounter God's splendor. As long as we're content to stare into the darkness, we'll never turn and see the light. But there, on the horizon, is the light of new possibilities, just waiting for us to take a closer look.

God is a horizon, not a box. He is visible from any vantage point in life. You don't have to land in the right box to see him. In fact, the horizon looks fragmented and small when you're trying to see it through a crack in a box. But bust open the box and step outside, and you will see a wide, amazing horizon that the box had been obscuring.

Any description of a horizon from one fixed point—including mine—is incomplete. The description of a horizon is complete only when the horizon has been seen from every vantage point—from the sea, from the air, and even from outer space.

God's the same way. Only when we have encountered him from every possible vantage point (which is impossible) will we fully comprehend him. In other words, when it comes to understanding God, most of us are ignorant.

But that's no reason to stop looking. God allows himself to be seen, which allows us to take a closer look. He's complex enough and mysterious enough to transcend every human attempt to explain him. But he's available enough to be experienced and known by us. Not perfectly, but authentically.

This isn't agnosticism; it's simply recognizing the fact that if we're going to really talk about God, we need to talk about *God* and not our limited view or experience of him. Let's find him on the horizon, not sitting inside a box.

HOW MUCH HORIZON DO YOU SEE?

One of the greatest uses of a horizon is to help airplanes stay level. A pilot can set the balance of his or her aircraft by the horizon. No matter where an airplane is in the sky, a pilot can take one look at the horizon and know where he or she is in relation to the earth. If all the pilot sees is sky, he or she knows that the plane is climbing. If all he or she sees is ground, the pilot knows the plane is in trouble.

In the same way, God is a leveling horizon to us. As we look out to the horizon that is God, we know immediately whether our view of life is balanced or imbalanced. God gives us the capacity to see where we stand in relationship to him. Many of us interpret life and eternal things in light of our obstructed view, in which only a fraction of the horizon is in sight. As a result, we never see the bigger picture of God or life. I've found that there is nothing more freeing than flying with as full a view of the horizon in front of me as is humanly possible.

In the Hebrew scriptures (also known as the Old Testament in the Bible), God asked Jonah to deliver the message of forgiveness to the enemy city of Nineveh. Jonah was reluctant to go because his view of the horizon allowed only for anger and bitterness toward his enemies. So he tried to bail out of the mission, only to be tracked by God. What Jonah didn't see was that God's horizon included plans of grace and restoration for those in Nineveh. Jonah nearly missed God's actual plan because of his limited view. It took a few nights in the belly of a giant fish for Jonah to straighten out his view.

I wonder what we might be missing out on because we're willing to look only at a small stretch of the wide horizon. I wonder what surprising things God would show us if we were willing to gaze into the full expanse of the horizon.

Your Turn to Talk

Now it's your turn to talk. Consider the following questions and then jot down your thoughts in a separate journal.

From what vantage point have you tended to view God? What limits and conditions have you placed on him? And how have those limits affected your view of him?

One more question (does this guy ever shut up?): Are you willing to lay down your limits for the remainder of our conversation and look at the horizon?

GOD DOESN'T WEAR CAMOUFLAGE

Is God at War or Is He Scheduling Peace Talks?

Have you ever noticed the difference between the image of American political figures and those from nations like Libya or Cuba? Americans like their politicians to look as apple-pie-and-ice-cream as possible. You know the look: Hart, Schaffner and Marx suits (the classic American single-breasted cut), diagonal-striped ties (preferably from Brooks Brothers), and no accessories or facial hair.

On the other hand, the citizens of Libya and Cuba are accustomed to seeing their leaders in camouflage. In countries where war and upheaval are commonplace, no one is alarmed when a politician looks as if he just stepped off the battlefield. But can you imagine public reaction in the United States if our president were to deliver the State of the Union address wearing olive drab, a beret, and combat boots?

Politicians aside, camouflage became fashionable in 2000 and 2001, even for Western civilians. Major designer fashions featured the camouflage look. From underwear to evening wear, camouflage was high fashion.

Then there's rocker and avid hunter Ted Nugent. The Nuge made plans to perform on a stage set that looked like a bunker lifted from the Iraqi desert. Camouflage, netting, sandbags, guns, and an inflatable

Sadaam (that got an arrow through the heart) served as the backdrop for Nugent's concerts. (You can read all about it on Ted's Web site, where you can also purchase an authentic Nuge camouflage cowboy hat.)

Camouflage is not just a tool of war; it's an image, a symbol, a metaphor. It's meant not only to blind enemies to your location but also to intimidate them. When you see somebody dressed in camouflage—whether it's a soldier, a dictator, a hunter, or Ted Nugent—you don't think of Hallmark cards and Disneyland. You think of war and, ultimately, of death.

It's disappointing that in many people's eyes, God wears camouflage. For as long as history has been recorded, religion has often sparked war and death. As a result, many see "God" as someone who brings war. Even Jesus's first followers were expecting Jesus to be a military commander who would lead the charge against the occupying Roman army. They weren't expecting a Prince of Peace. They definitely weren't expecting a low-key rabbi who would sacrifice his own life for his people.

Suicide attacks in Israel and other parts of the Middle East, and terrorist acts in the United States, Europe, and Asia, remind us that religion and war are a lethal combination. And the perceptions of cause-and-effect work both ways. It's easy for Americans to see the violent acts of militant Muslims as attacks not only on Western capitalism and cultural vices but also against those who hold Christian beliefs. Likewise, it's not difficult for Muslims living in Afghanistan or Iraq to read religious imperialism into the occupying American military forces. I've heard people say that U.S. efforts to combat terrorism are actually expressions of hatred toward the Islamic world. Soon after the towers of the World Trade Center fell in 2001, we had an eerie sense that we had just witnessed the first major volley in an expanding religious war.

During the Middle Ages, Pope Urban II (the avowed head of the Western church)[1] campaigned to unite the various competing armies of Christian Europe in a crusade to liberate Jerusalem and the Holy Land

from the Muslims. The pope blessed the Crusades, and knights journeyed to the Middle East to join what they perceived to be a fight against
the enemies of God. The church sanctioned the killing of Muslims and
other so-called infidels and heretics. Untold numbers of Muslim men,
women, and children were butchered. The crusaders also killed Jews and
great numbers of non-Latin Christians. But the sword also turned against
the invading armies, and most of the crusaders never returned to their
homelands. They were slaughtered just as they had slaughtered others,
thinking they were fighting for Christ and his church. After nearly two
hundred years of unspeakable bloodshed, the Crusades failed when Muslims recaptured Jerusalem and the rest of the Holy Land. However, the
Crusades caused gaping wounds in Muslim-Christian relations that have
yet to be healed.

In 1999 leaders from Buddhist, Christian (Old Catholic, Orthodox,
Protestant, and Roman Catholic), Jewish, and Muslim faith traditions
met in Geneva, Switzerland, to address the problem of religion and violence. The delegates claimed that fifty-six current wars, civil disturbances,
and other armed conflicts have significant religious elements—escalating
from religious strife to armed violence. In the past thirty years, they said,
such conflicts around the world have numbered in the thousands.[2]

What good is religion if it promotes bloodshed rather than harmony?
Is religion only good for those who happen to agree with the group that
has the biggest guns? You've probably asked this question yourself. I know
I have.

AND IN THIS CORNER...

Hate and religious war are antithetical to the beliefs and practices of anyone who is authentically pursuing God. So-called religious wars almost
always result from someone's attempt to limit God—to put him in their
corner and at their service against their enemies. God does not lead his

people like the manager of a World Wrestling Entertainment (WWE) wrestler, shouting "Crush that piece of trash!" as he looks at the supposed bad guy in the opposite corner.

That's just not what God is like.

Some of Jesus's earliest followers had to learn this lesson. Many of them thought God loved only the Jews. Bear in mind, most of Jesus's first followers were Jews themselves. Because God had maintained a special relationship with the nation of Israel for thousands of years, they concluded that God was in their corner to the exclusion of non-Jews. So when Jesus came to bring salvation to humanity, many of them believed it applied only to the Jews.

But then God told one of Jesus's followers, Simon Peter, to go and tell a Gentile (a non-Jew) named Cornelius how Jesus came from heaven to earth so that "everyone who believes in him receives forgiveness of sins through his name."[3] Simon Peter realized that God was not just in the Jews' corner. I love what Simon Peter said to Cornelius: "God plays no favorites! It makes no difference who you are or where you're from—if you want God and are ready to do as he says, the door is open."[4] God made it clear that he is pro-people, whoever they are. He is not swayed by the issues that divide one group from another. He wants everyone— Jew, Gentile, Muslim, European, Asian, male, female, aboriginal, Pacific Islander—to find him.[5]

It's difficult for a WWE culture to grasp a God who's cheering for people on *both* sides. Many people find it uncomfortable to look past the things we use to create opposing sides, the things that help us separate friends from enemies. God does have views on issues, and not everyone is right in God's eyes. But a person's views, politics, and faith commitments don't automatically turn God against him or her. And what a person swears allegiance to today really says nothing about that person's future commitments. As we'll see in later chapters, God is constantly at work revealing himself and making his love known so that we can see past falsehood and embrace him not only as our Creator but as our Savior and our Lord.

WHAT PEACE LOOKS LIKE

Jesus, who is God made visible to us, provided a living demonstration of God's impartiality, to the dismay of the religious leaders of his day. When others saw a whore who deserved to be stoned, Jesus saw a woman who needed forgiveness. When others viewed a certain woman as subhuman because of her immorality, religious convictions, and gender, Jesus saw a woman who needed his personal attention. When others saw the Samaritan people as an inferior, mongrel race, Jesus invited the Samaritans to follow him and join his spiritual family. When others despised the tax-collection agency of Jesus's day and called the IRS agents "sinners," Jesus ate dinner with them. When Jesus came across people who believed much differently than he did, he didn't automatically condemn them. At times, he went into their homes and shared a meal with them. When people tried to keep children away from Jesus because kids were a hassle, Jesus invited children to come to him. He affirmed their value in his kingdom. When the rich were catered to because they could donate large sums of money to the temple treasury, Jesus affirmed the heart of a widow who had hardly anything to give but gave everything she had.[6]

These compelling scenes teach something significant about God: He rarely joins human causes. It's not that he's not interested; it's just that he sees people much differently than we do. We define and categorize people according to *what we think they are*—then we decide either to side with them or against them. God sees people for what they *will be* and chooses to love them now despite their present condition.

A number of years ago, I received a call from a friend. Jim had been rushed to the emergency room after an overdose. Someone at a party had slipped something into Jim's drink as a harmless prank. But instead of being harmless, the substance had caused Jim to have a severe reaction, and he was now fighting for his life.

A few days later I went to see Jim after he had been moved to a psych ward. In my nonmedical opinion, Jim's brain had been fried. I wasn't sure what would become of him. But over time, during a process of healing physically, spiritually, and emotionally, Jim found a relationship with Jesus Christ. The transformation, while slow, was consistent and dramatic. He was able to finish college and earn two master's degrees.

I had thought all was lost, but God knew things were just beginning. We can only see where people are; God sees where they're going. And that's why we can't give up on anyone or turn against them—no matter how bad things seem.

ONE PIECE AT A TIME

People don't just wake up one morning and decide that God has turned into a divine warlord, firing a rifle into the air and threatening his enemies with certain destruction. Instead, people dress God in camouflage one piece at a time over a long period of time. The sequence of thoughts might look something like this:

- *God is only on our side.*
- *I can see that you're not on God's side.*
- *That makes you God's enemy.*
- *Since you're God's enemy, that makes you my enemy.*
- *It's my duty to punish you for being God's enemy.*
- *God is pleased when I attack and defeat his enemies.*
- *When I defeat God's enemies, I'm pleased with myself.*

People who think this way feel best about themselves when they are waging war against God's "enemies." This leads not only to unholy religious wars but also to the commonplace pride and arrogance that is prevalent among those who are the most religious. I'm not a pacifist in the strictest sense of the word. I don't protest every war, and I don't object to people fighting to defend their country and protect their families when the cause is just. But when people take up guns, bombs, and battle plans to advance their version of the cause of God, they have a basic misunderstanding of God and what he is all about.

The same is true when people resort to various forms of unarmed warfare—infighting, wars of words, and hatred. They misunderstand God's basic characteristic: love. In fact, one of the New Testament writers in the Bible said that "God is love."[7]

When religious people divide the world into "us" and "them," they typically resort to hate rather than love. As I read the newspapers and listen to the religious tone of our day, I hear a lot of culture-war language, much of it springing from people in my own religious circle. I hear slogans such as "Put God Back in America" and "Fight for What's Right." In many cases, such warlike mottoes center on moral and social issues such as abortion, stem-cell research, vouchers for private schools, gay marriage, and prayer in public schools. Many of today's religious "heroes" are those who speak the most stridently against groups they believe are "enemies of the Christian ethic."

Moral crusades and culture wars can easily mushroom into physical violence. When some opponents of abortion grow weary of or frustrated with nonviolent resistance, they resort to bombing abortion clinics and even shooting abortion doctors. Paul Hill, a professing Christian, justified his killing of an abortion doctor with the rationale that he was saving innocent babies from being aborted. When Hill was executed for his crime, his supporters said he was "martyred." Hill himself said, "I expect a great reward in heaven.... I am looking forward to glory."[8]

Christians who kill non-Christians are nothing new. But most of the wars carried out in the name of Jesus have been between Christians. The longstanding history of bloodshed between Roman Catholics and Protestants is a huge embarrassment Christians have to deal with.[9] In the seventeenth century, these two Christian groups fought the Thirty Years War (AD 1618–48), one of the bloodiest wars in Europe's history. During the early period of Roman Catholic missionary work in South America, the natives were forced, often at the point of a sword, to confess faith in Jesus Christ. Then, after the natives were baptized, their heads were lopped off. In England many Catholic or Protestant heads rolled, literally, in the name of Jesus, depending upon the religious allegiance of the king or queen. This tradition is still carried on, albeit a bit differently, in Northern Ireland, where members of these two groups still kill one another.

Here's the deal: God doesn't wear battle fatigues—at least not yet. The idea of God is not meant to be proved or debated on a battlefield. The only exception to this that I can find is in the Old Testament of the Bible, where God on many occasions commanded the Israelite people to kill non-Israelite enemies—and even at times one another.

For example, in Exodus 32, the people of Israel made a golden calf to represent God. They burned sacrifices and worshiped before this idol. However, God had strictly prohibited them from channeling their worship through such images.[10] So Moses, whom God had appointed to lead Israel, divided the people into "us" and "them"—those who wanted to obey God strictly, and those who didn't. Once he divided the people, he said to those who wanted to obey God: "Each man strap a sword to his side. Go back and forth through the camp from one end to the other, each killing his brother and friend and neighbor."[11] About three thousand people were killed that day.

I believe the Bible is a true account of God's actions and his desires for us, but I don't get this part. The best I can tell is that God was trying to establish that he was God (with a capital G) and not just some two-bit tribal deity. By commanding the people of Israel to declare their allegiance, and then to render judgment on those who wanted to keep their options open, he was displaying his power in a very tangible way. It was also to show that God was not a solo act. He had a people, and their name was Israel. God's blessings and curses followed this people. This does not explain everything, I know. Because in the New Testament, Jesus forbids hating your enemy and cursing those who curse you. He even commanded his followers to pray for people who abused them. Jesus said: God "causes his sun to rise on the evil and the good, and sends rain on the righteous and the unrighteous."[12] And that's not all. He continued: "If you greet only your brothers, what are you doing more than others? Do not even pagans do that? Be perfect, therefore, as your heavenly Father is perfect."[13]

Although God demonstrated his justice in the past by violent means, he has always been a God of love and grace. God's people are no longer to be marked as a military force with whom everyone else must reckon. God and his people are forever a community profoundly marked by love. Jesus taught that these are the people who are blessed:

> Blessed are the poor in spirit,
> for theirs is the kingdom of heaven.
> Blessed are those who mourn,
> for they will be comforted.
> Blessed are the meek,
> for they will inherit the earth.
> Blessed are those who hunger and thirst for righteousness,
> for they will be filled.
> Blessed are the merciful,
> for they will be shown mercy.
> Blessed are the pure in heart,
> for they will see God.
> Blessed are the peacemakers,
> for they will be called sons of God.

Blessed are those who are persecuted because of righteousness,
> for theirs is the kingdom of heaven.[14]

This sounds nothing at all like the religious army-fatigue mentality. I see nothing of "Blessed are you when you blow up those with whom you disagree. Blessed are you when you speak poison about your enemies and run them into the ground." Yet, interestingly, faith communities often reward those who display the camouflage mentality while rejecting those who challenge them with the words of Jesus. There is a big difference between being "combative" and being corrective.

WHERE DO YOU SEE GOD?

The Bible tells us that no person has seen God, but we do see evidence of him in the world.[15] Many say they see evidence of God in the mind-boggling expanse of the universe, in the deafening roar of the ocean, in the breathtaking beauty of a sunset, in the intricacy of a spider web, in the beauty of the human body, in natural wonders such as the Grand Canyon. And even in supernatural phenomena.

All of these things allude to a God who not only loves intricacy and mystery but is incredibly powerful and smart. Even the songwriters of the Old Testament (called psalmists) were captivated by God's awesome creation. One of them wrote,

> The LORD reigns, let the earth be glad;
>> let the distant shores rejoice.
> Clouds and thick darkness surround him;
>> righteousness and justice are the foundation of his throne....
> His lightning lights up the world;
>> the earth sees and trembles.
> The mountains melt like wax before the LORD,

> before the Lord of all the earth.
> The heavens proclaim his righteousness,
>   and all the peoples see his glory.[16]

But creation alone does not give us the whole picture of God—or even the best picture. In fact, if you see God only in the power and majesty of creation, you've missed him. Even more, you may well be on your way to dressing God in camouflage.

The Bible tells us that God is not seen most clearly in the splendor of nature, in the most powerful and forceful parts of the world. He is seen most clearly in the life and teachings of Jesus Christ, who was God in human form. In particular, God was most visible hanging on a contraption of death called a cross, shedding his blood for us. We see most clearly what God is like in his suffering, not in his splendor. Listen to what one of Jesus's early followers said: "For the message of the cross is foolishness to those who are perishing, but to us who are being saved it is the power of God.… For the foolishness of God is wiser than man's wisdom, and the weakness of God is stronger than man's strength."[17]

God shows us his power most clearly in suffering. He shows us his wisdom in what the world considers foolishness. When God wanted to give the final word on what he was like, he gave us Jesus, who suffered and died. And Jesus said, "If you really knew me, you would know my Father as well. From now on, you do know him and have seen him.… Anyone who has seen me has seen the Father."[18] Jesus was telling his followers, "If you want to see what God is like, just look at me."

It's easy for people to miss this. When we think of God, we don't think of suffering, persecution, shame, and death. We think of majesty, power, and strength. A medieval German monk named Martin Luther called this "the Theology of the Cross versus the Theology of Glory." In his *Heidelberg Disputation,* theses 19–20, Luther briefly described his theology of the cross. He understood the human tendency to want to look for God in all the powerful and beautiful things in life. In fact, an ancient leader of Israel, Moses, once demanded of God, "Show me your glory."[19] In making that demand, Moses meant, "Show me how big, strong, and magnificent you are!"

But Martin Luther made the point that looking for God in "glory" is looking in the wrong place. Even though God can be seen in ocean waves, the broad expanse of sky, and nature in general,[20] this isn't where he's seen most clearly. To see God clearly you must see him hanging on a cross, dying. You must see him suffering, hiding his strength in weakness, and concealing his glory in shame. To miss the suffering and shame of God on the cross is to misunderstand God.

I enjoy the beauty of nature as much as anyone. However, I also understand that a preoccupation with God's strength in nature at the expense of seeing his shame on the cross ultimately leads to disaster. So long as people see God as the master powerbroker, they will believe that they must overpower others on his behalf. If God's ultimate characteristic is power, then his followers will see ample reason to use power to advance his cause on earth.

One of Jesus's first followers, Simon Peter, mixed this up. When a mob came to arrest Jesus, Peter drew a sword and cut off one guy's ear. In fact, all of Jesus's closest followers were ready to draw their swords and fight for the one they loved. I probably would have done the same thing.

But Jesus's response was remarkable. He told Simon Peter, "Put your sword back in its place,…for all who draw the sword will die by the sword. Do you think I cannot call on my Father, and he will at once put at my disposal more than twelve legions of angels?"[21] Jesus did not and does not need people to fight his battles for him. He can easily handle things on his own, if that's what he needs to do. What Jesus needs from his followers, then and now, is commitment to an alternative way of advancing the Kingdom of God: through love.

God's ultimate characteristic is sacrificial love, which is seen in his suffering. Therefore, his cause must be advanced by sacrificial love. This is why religious war, bloody or not, is fatally flawed. If God advanced his cause through humility and love, shame and sacrifice, then those are the only weapons his followers can legitimately use. God's followers influence others through sacrificial love. This is how God wants to be noticed and experienced.

GOD'S TOWEL

If God does not wear camouflage, what does he wear? Surprisingly, he wears a towel.

On the evening before Jesus was executed, he did something unexpected. Since he knew his enemies were plotting to kill him, you'd expect him to don fatigues, call together a couple billion angels, sharpen his sword, and prepare for battle.

But instead, Jesus filled a basin with water, got out a towel, and washed his followers' filthy feet. He became their servant. Rather than displaying power and force, Jesus modeled humility and gentleness. But the story intensifies. After Jesus washed his followers' feet, he said, "Now that I, your Lord and Teacher, have washed your feet, you also should wash one another's feet. I have set you an example that you should do as I have done for you."[22] His followers are to be associated with servanthood, not war. When we can't get along, we continue to serve. When we disagree, we remain humble. When we don't get our way, we still submit. When we're hated, we show love. Those are images of Jesus's followers—both in the first century and today.

Some would say, "You're never going to get very far that way." And in some ways, they're right. Jesus and most of his closest original followers (called the apostles) laid down their lives. They didn't even declare a culture war. They took the attitude of a servant, just like Jesus did. However, I would say they accomplished a lot. They changed the world. Jesus's subsequent disciples have withstood persecution for two thousand years, and Christianity continues to thrive. The best human attempts to snuff out Jesus's followers have failed miserably. In fact, it seems that the more persecution Jesus's followers face, the more they thrive.

So what should people who have deep religious convictions, Christians especially, do when they disagree with others? They need to take off the camouflage and put on a towel. And the place to begin applying Jesus's example of servanthood is in our conversations about faith. A faith conversation should be relationship, not war. It's carried in the words of dialogue and in the efforts of honest understanding.

Your Turn to Talk

I just threw a lot at you in one chapter. But I'm curious about this: Have you been bothered by religious people who insist on dressing God in camouflage?

How do you react to my statements that we see God most clearly in suffering rather than in power? Also, how did you first hear about God?

Write your thoughts and questions in your journal.

DROP INTO THE BOWL

God Is More Extreme Than Anything We Can Imagine

Extreme sports are taking the sports-crazed world by storm. Kids used to get excited about watching people try to hit a baseball out of a grass park. But today's younger generation is far more enthralled with mountain biking, jibbing, Freestyle Moto-X, skateboarding, snowboarding, surfing, kiteboarding, and Jet Ski racing. There's even an Extreme Sports Channel *(www.extreme.com)* where you can catch the thrill of extreme sports 24/7.

This extreme trend excites me. Traditional sports were all about staying inbounds, working within the rules, developing a better strategy, and accepting the limits imposed by gravity. Extreme sports are all about pushing the limits and defying gravity. They're about juicing up the risk by making the human body—not a ball or a puck—the thing that hurls through the air. They're not so much about strategy as they are about just going for it, whatever it takes. Extreme athletes do what everybody else says can't or shouldn't be done.

Limits? Boundaries? Confinement? What are they?

You may be thinking, *I thought Christians and God were all about control and obeying the rules. What's the deal?* In some circles, those who believe in God think it's most important to define the rules and then make sure everybody toes the line. If you've ever been around that brand of Christian, you know that conformity is valued above just about any-thing else. Nothing risky. Nothing extreme. Yawn.

But God is anything but ordinary or boring. He's not standard issue, he's not routine, he's not completely predictable, and he doesn't conform to any rules but his own. The more I discover about God, the more I see the disparity between most people's views of God (that he is rote, narrow, ordinary) and his actual personality and activity, which are intensely, incredibly extraordinary.[1]

EXTREME GOD

Extreme living wasn't invented by enthusiasts of extreme sports. Risky living is the most ancient thing I've read about. Thales of Miletus, a Greek philosopher and mathematician who lived from 640 to 546 BC, said it all when he wrote, "Shun security." Little did he know that he was affirming an aspect of God's nature.

God is one who pushes the limits. He does what nobody thinks can or should be done. Every day he shows up in people's lives in extreme ways. God is someone who does the impossible, breaks barriers, defies the laws of nature to accomplish his goals. One of the writers of the Bible—Paul—left us with one of my favorite descriptions of God: "Now to him who is able to do immeasurably more than all we ask or imag-ine…"[2] Do me a favor; read that sentence again. Now answer this ques-tion: Does this sound like a God of the ordinary? Hardly.

As the Gospels record, Jesus pushed the limits of just about every law of nature. He healed diseases. He raised people from the dead, and he was raised from the dead himself. He commanded the wind and the sea to be still, and they obeyed him. He turned water into wine. He fed thousands of people with a few loaves of bread and a few fish. He told evil spirits to come out of people, and they obeyed him. Those who knew him would never have described Jesus as being ordinary.

I'm convinced that our human tendency to test limits, to chafe against routine, and to look for more than just the ordinary reflects an inner sense that there is a God in the universe who exceeds all limits. When I see people pushing limits, I see God in them. However, people tend to short-circuit this connection to God by not allowing their extreme tendencies to be directed toward God himself. So instead, we channel our extreme tendencies into self-destructive excesses, such as drugs, alcohol, food, money, sex, power, and career. We go wild in these areas because something in us drives us to extremes. But we don't realize that the big extreme we're seeking is God. I've learned by experience that only God can fill our inner drive for extreme living.

For me, pushing the limits happens on my Harley. I choose to ride mostly on open country roads. I do this not just so I can "open it up" but also so I can feel every nuance of this powerful machine. Many people like to escape to a quiet place where they can sit by a placid lake or get lost in the mountains to enjoy absolute quiet and feel the presence of God. Not me! I feel God on my Harley. Wide open. Wind whipping. The deafening rumble of those pipes. It feels extraordinary to me, and that's where I feel God. It's where I remember that following Jesus is a radical lifestyle, not passive conformity. My Harley calls me back to my spiritual roots.

GOD OF THE RISKTAKER

In a talk called "A World at Risk," Leonard Sweet described a new skate park that opened on Orcas Island in the San Juan Islands off the coast of Washington. Parents were thrilled their children had a place to hang out. In the first four days after the skate park opened, the Orcas Island Medical Center, located just a block away, saw seven fractured arms and wrists. By the end of the summer, the broken-bone count averaged three per week. And that doesn't include all the broken teeth that the local dentist handled. Some kids wore all their safety equipment and still got mangled. Other kids skated with only a helmet.[3] But nobody stayed away because it was too "dangerous." The kids knew they had to drop into the bowl (a stomach-twisting twelve-foot drop into a big cement bowl) if they wanted to get better at their sport. They had to risk it all.

Something about risk moves the human spirit. Humans are enthralled with putting it all on the line for the sake of a cause they believe in, even when they're not sure of the outcome. The cause could be skateboarding, venturing a start-up software company, or space travel. When it comes to humanity, it seems the greater the risk, the more we like it.

It's interesting that we appear to be designed for faith, which the Bible defines as "the substance of things hoped for, the evidence of things not seen."[4] Faith is what it takes to face risk. Life would be pretty robotic if we acted only on things that had a guaranteed positive outcome.

Maybe you think your life is pretty settled. You get up, go to work and/or school, come home, eat dinner, watch television, and go to bed. Even if this is a typical day for you, it's still full of more risk than you can imagine. Consider the risks we face in any given year:

- One in every 437,212 Americans will die this year in a fall from a bed, chair, or other piece of household furniture. Those odds are not far from the chance a few years ago of being killed by the two snipers who were operating in the Washington DC area (1 chance in 344,000).[5]
- Your chance of being killed in a car accident? 1 in 18,752.
- Your chance of being killed by accidental poisoning? 1 in 22,388.
- Your chance of being murdered with a gun? 1 in 25,196.
- Your chance of being killed by accidental drowning? 1 in 77,308.

- Your chance of being killed by lightning? 1 in 4,262,813 (yet most of us stay indoors when there's lightning—where we're more likely to be killed by furniture).
- You are fifteen times more likely to die from a natural cause (like a disease or old age) than from external causes like a car accident, shooting, or drowning. [6]

Despite these risks, people think nothing of jumping out of bed, getting into a car, diving into a swimming pool, or just generally being out in public. Even the drabbest life is an extreme sport. I believe God designed things so that we can't possibly lead a risk-free life, even if we wanted to. Risk puts us in touch with God because it forces us (even when we don't know it) to live by faith.

PERSONAL THREAT MATRIX

Nearly every day the president of the United States is apprised of all the people and issues that threaten the safety of our nation. It's called the threat matrix. So I got to thinking about my personal threat matrix—all the things my life depends on but are outside my control. Any one of these, at any time, has the potential to wipe me from the face of the earth. Here are a few of the threats that made it onto my matrix:

- the air I breathe
- any movement of the earth closer to the sun
- the water I drink
- any one of a large number of natural disasters, such as tornadoes, hurricanes, earthquakes, and fires
- lethal bacteria that floats around freely in the air
- the guy driving on the other side of the road
- the wiring in my house
- the people who work in the kitchen of the restaurant where I buy fast food

As I think about this list, I can either get paranoid and never leave my house (where I still have a decent chance of getting killed), or I can do the reasonable thing and live by faith. Self-preservation isn't possible because the odds are stacked too heavily against us. Human survival is a sheer act of faith. But most people don't perceive their need to trust God because they refuse to recognize their own vulnerability. They haven't been briefed on their threat matrix.

A MODEL RISKTAKER

Let's talk about a big-time risktaker named Rahab, a prostitute who lived in the city of Jericho some thirty-four hundred years ago. Two Israelite spies happened on to her house when they were scoping out the city as Israel made plans to sack it. She allowed them to stay in her home, but word of the spies got out to the king of the city. Rahab hid the spies on her roof and then told the soldiers who came by that the spies had already left. Risk number one.

Then, knowing the spies intended to return with Israel's army to destroy her people, Rahab pleaded with them to spare her life and the lives of her family. The spies told her to hang a red cord from her window, which would be the sign to the attacking army not to harm those in that house. And get this: The spies were the enemy, but she believed them. Risk number two.

She gathered her family and stayed in the house knowing that an army was going to return to annihilate the city. Risk number three (now she's risking the lives of other people).

What was the outcome, you ask? The spies were true to their word, and the house of Rahab was spared.[7] And catch this: God honored the life of Rahab, the prostitute and risktaker. She became part of the family line that would eventually produce Jesus.[8]

Risktakers are those who birth God's purposes in this world.

A QUICK DIGRESSION (BUT NOT THE LAST)

May I digress long enough to ask a somewhat personal question? What risks are you taking to accomplish something that will advance a bigger cause than your own livelihood? How is your life being spent for the good of others?

I won't ask you a question without revealing some things in my own life. When I was the pastor of Calvary Church, I risked a lot for the purpose of unity in the church. The church is way too divided by race, denominations, and differing views about such issues as spiritual gifts, the "last days," and even more minor issues, such as worship styles. I put a lot on the line personally to do something to heal this disunity. For example, although I led a primarily white church in a prominent southern city, I developed a multicultural staff. Trust me when I tell you that this was risky. I also tried to bring our city churches together for shared worship and ministry. Despite the little things that separated us, we had a common faith in one Lord—Jesus Christ. Again, in our city this was relatively uncharted territory.

God wants me to go where others have chosen not to go. He wants me to have faith in him to the extent that I will trade status-quo living for extraordinary living. I'm also learning that when I risk something big—like my reputation or my livelihood or opposition from other religious leaders—I find incredible connectedness to God. I feel him saying, "Glenn, this is what I created you for—the life of full-bore faith in my ability to do more than you can imagine."

Your Turn to Talk

Biblical Christianity is an extreme sport because God is an extreme God. I want my belief about God's limitlessness to show up in how I live. I want God to be more than just words. God is worth whatever risks I take for him.

How about you? If you could be doing anything right now, what would it be? Do you believe God is ready for whatever challenge you might lay before him?

What's important here is that you're processing this conversation through your personal grid. Maybe you don't even believe there is a God. Maybe you don't buy my take on what God is like. Or maybe you're mostly okay with what has been said so far, and you're ready to move on. Wherever you're at, take things at your own pace. Take some time and record your thoughts in your journal.

GOD LIKES STUFF

Your Invitation into the Shameless Enjoyment of Life

W e've spent quite a bit of time talking about what God is like, so let's shift gears and in the next few chapters talk about the things God really likes.

A lot of people think of God as a grumpy old man who bans fun and enjoyment and likes it best when we're stuck in a rut. I have found him to be just the opposite. He's a God who likes stuff, and I've found a lot of happiness as I've gotten involved with the stuff God likes.

But God has gotten a bad rap. I can't count the number of people I've talked with who think of God as someone who doesn't like stuff. They picture a God who doesn't like fun or beauty or much of anything.

It's no wonder that so many of God's followers are so negative. They dislike far more things than they like. Their identity is shaped more by what they oppose than by what they favor. Know anyone like that? Yeah, me too.

Dana Carvey was successful with his church-lady routine on *Saturday Night Live* because it was so dead-on. Church ladies and their male counterparts are cynical, judgmental, and sanctimonious. While these types of people are certainly not the norm, they often come to mind when people picture a typical Christian.

How would this change if more Christians saw God as someone who actually likes stuff? I mean, that he actually *enjoys* things. Not just saints and angels, but art, music, film, virtue, love, and life in general. Well, this isn't just fantasy; God really does like stuff, because, as C. S. Lewis said, "God invented matter."[1]

GOD IS NOT A GNOSTIC

Gnosticism is an ancient belief that is fundamentally opposed to the material world. Its goal is escaping the hard realities of the physical realm and entering the bliss of the spiritual world—the only world that really matters. Much of the spirituality of our day has a distinctly Gnostic bent. From New Age mystic spirituality that teaches mind over matter to fundamentalist Christian spirituality that calls adherents to be separate from "the world," I see Gnosticism everywhere. I guess it's not so ancient after all.[2]

Dr. Eric Voegelin, a political scientist at the University of Munich, regards our era as "the revival of Gnosticism." He says, "The world is no longer the…Judeo-Christian world that God created and found good. Gnostic man no longer wishes to perceive in admiration the intrinsic order of the cosmos. For him the world has become a prison from which he wants to escape."[3] In such a culture, God is considered distant from our world. He rarely intrudes, not because he is unable to, but because he doesn't care.

But this is a far cry from the picture of God we find in the Bible. In the book of Genesis, we find God as the one who actually created the physical world. The world as we know it is God's design. From the vastness of the universe to the intricacy of the subatomic world, God's fingerprints are all over the physical realm.[4] But there's more to the story.

After taking a good look at everything he created (including the earth, the human body, and the animal world), God realized "it was very good."[5] Nothing about the physical world, as God made it, displeased him. He affirmed its worth and commissioned humans to care for it because it was good.[6] Matter mattered, not because of its intrinsic value, but because it bore the fingerprint of God.

The apostle Paul said, "For since the creation of the world God's invisible qualities—his eternal power and divine nature—have been clearly seen, being understood from what has been made."[7] By looking at what God made, we learn more about what God is like. This is why matter is "very good." It's also why life and the earth itself must be protected and preserved. Humanity bears the image of God, and the universe bears the fingerprint of God.

If creation itself is good, so is life within that creation. God actually likes it when we enjoy what he has made, and when we use his creation as he intended. John Calvin, a sixteenth-century Christ-follower, said it this way: "Being placed in this most beautiful theater, let us not decline to take a pious delight in the clear and manifest works of God."[8]

The world a theater? Delight in creation? Shameless enjoyment of life? This does not sound like the religion of our day, does it? But this is how God sees the world he made. God is not a Gnostic.

CULTURE'S THREE FACES

White light refracts into the three primary colors of red, yellow, and blue. These three can theoretically be mixed to produce all the other colors; the primary colors combine to color the world. God's enjoyment of the world is similar. There are three primary sources of enjoyment God has in what he has made, which can combine into an endless assortment of things God likes.

God's three primary sources of pleasure are truth, beauty, and goodness. Everything God likes in us or in any other part of creation or culture can be boiled down to one of these three, or ideally a combination of the three.

If you're looking for stuff God likes, here are the questions to ask: What reflects God's order and design (truth)? What reflects God's perfection and symmetry (beauty)? What reflects God's virtue and character (goodness)? Looking for God in all that's true, all that's beautiful, and all that's good has helped me enjoy the world and, ultimately, enjoy God himself.

When it comes to art, I enjoy the vividness of Rembrandt, the softness of Monet, and the life-in-action of Renoir. My maternal grandfather, a professional musician, taught me to love and appreciate all forms and styles of music. So I enjoy classical music and a lot of contemporary music as well. But I really gravitate toward jazz and the blues—artists like Maynard Ferguson, Miles Davis, and the real king, B. B. King. Art and music draw my soul closer to God because they embody so much of what God enjoys.

It's important to realize that truth, beauty, and goodness go together. One leads to the other. When something is true, it's also beautiful and good. When something is beautiful, it reflects what's true and good. God does not take pleasure in one at the expense of the others.

I've seen people limit their view of the world to only one of these three values. Scientists and technocrats see the world from a mechanistic perspective and often neglect beauty and virtue. They're likely to get excited about the discovery of a new star or the invention of a faster computer platform, but they don't get excited about going to the latest exhibit at the art museum. What matters to these people is hard facts. They remind me of Thomas Gradgrind in Charles Dickens's novel *Hard Times,* who said, "Teach these boys and girls Facts. Nothing but Facts. Facts alone are wanted in life. Plant nothing else, and root out everything else. You can only form the minds of reasoning animals upon Facts: nothing else will ever be of any service to them."[9]

Artists can easily make the opposite mistake. They can fixate on sensory expression but often neglect pursuing truth. They're jazzed by taking art classes, playing or listening to music, or reading and writing literature, but they are pathetically bored by mathematics, chemistry, or geology.

Moralists can top both of the other groups in the practice of neglect. They see only what's "right" from their perspective. Moralists believe they must like or agree with something in order to justify its existence. They're interested not in what you've created or discovered but in whether you agree with them. They're the ones who, when looking at a piece of art, say, "I don't like it, so it was wrong for you to create it." Which makes me want to respond, "Who cares? The artist who created it was looking for a response, not necessarily agreement. It's meant to depict something in creation from the artist's perspective." Okay, I'll lighten up on the moralists.

What kind of person are you? Scientist, artist, or moralist? With my musical background and training, I can identify with the artist. My technical training enables me to understand the scientist, and my theological and philosophical education has tuned me in to the identity of the moralist.

How you see life has a lot to do with how you relate to God. None of the three types of values is bad, and we need all three. I suggest we start listening to each other more carefully so that we can help each other see aspects of God that we might otherwise ignore.

Here's where I'm going: God likes all three of these values and can be seen in all three. Life should be marked by the pursuit of truth, beauty, and goodness, even though we as individuals tend to favor one over the others. To live in relationship to God is not to deny enjoyment; it's recognizing ultimate joy and pursuing it with abandon. A contemporary Christ-follower named John Piper put it this way: "God is most glorified in us when we are most satisfied in Him."[10] To love God is to love joy at its most profound level. Blaise Pascal said it this way: "The infinite Abyss can only be filled by an infinite and immutable object, that is to say, only by God Himself."[11]

PLATO AND THE FINGERPRINT OF GOD

Philosophers, even nonreligious philosophers, have recognized the significance of the triad of truth, beauty, and goodness. It seems everybody realizes that life itself is good, whether or not they acknowledge God's pronouncement behind it.

The first recorded connection of truth, beauty, and goodness is found in the writings of Plato in the fourth century BC. Since the time of Plato, truth, beauty, and goodness were recognized as the primary values of Western culture. In his book *The Great Ideas: A Syntopicon of Great Books of the Western World,* philosopher Mortimer Adler makes the connection that the triad of truth, beauty, and goodness have been discussed together throughout the tradition of Western thought.[12] In support of his conclusions, Adler cites thinkers from Socrates to Freud who acknowledged the fundamental connection between truth, beauty, and goodness.

Virtually every spiritual tradition has also recognized these three values as primary spiritual realities. The Indian philosopher Sri Aurobindo describes three "dynamic images" through which a seeker makes contact with "supreme Reality":

- the way of the intellect or of knowledge—the way of Truth
- the way of the heart or of emotion—the way of Beauty
- the way of the will or of action—the way of Goodness[13]

Similarly, in *The Urantia Book* (claimed by adherents to have been authored by celestial beings and given by way of special revelation), beauty, truth, and goodness are identified as the material, intellectual, and spiritual manifestations of the Creator's love.[14]

In Western as well as Eastern thought, both Christian and non-Christian, much is made of the fact that certain realities of life—namely truth, beauty, and goodness—are valued above all others. And though philosophers from both sides of the world have acknowledged the essentially spiritual nature of this triad, they stop short of recognizing what makes these aspects of life so desirable. I want to suggest that it is the imprint and effect of God's fingerprint. That's what gives value and significance to truth, beauty, and goodness.

A SENSORY GOD

All of this points to something you may never have thought about: God is multisensory. He is fully observant and involved with the sensory world, so much so that he actually built into the world an incredible assortment of sensory wonders. Consider the things we learn about God by observing what he has made:

- The eyes of God love color. Most of God's creation contains color.
- The ears of God love sound. Just listen—is there really such a thing as complete silence?
- The hands of God love work. Nothing in God's creation comes easily.
- The heart of God loves virtue. Every culture has heroes.
- The mind of God loves intricacy. Nothing in God's creation is simple.

Thoughts such as these inspired David, a king and poet who lived in the Middle East around 1034–965 BC, to write:

The heavens declare the glory of God;
  the skies proclaim the work of his hands....
Their voice goes out into all the earth,
  their words to the ends of the world.[15]

Even a cursory look at what God has made leads us to conclude that he must have incredible taste. He is the ultimate artist, engineer, scientist, and moral example all in one. More and more, we need to come to see God as one who affirms, not condemns, our life in all its fullness.

GOD IN THE FLESH

God's pleasure in the world and in us goes even further than creation. Interestingly, many of the early church fathers (who were the first church leaders following the death of Jesus) argued against the Gnostics not on the basis of creation but by challenging them on the basis of incarnation. They tried to show that God demonstrated his pleasure and interest in the physical world by becoming a part of the physical world himself.

God became a man in Jesus. Through the Incarnation (God taking on human flesh), God was seen in his creation, and seeing him there was a good thing. John of Damascus, a theologian from the eighth century, said, "Previously there was absolutely no way in which God, who has neither a body nor a face, could be represented by any image. But now that he has made himself visible in the flesh and has lived with people, I can make an image of what I have seen of God...and contemplate the glory of the Lord, his face having been unveiled."[16]

Gregory Palamas, a Byzantine Christian, wrote something similar around the year 1335. He said, "Scripture shows us God descending from his supreme dwelling place and raising us up from our humble condition on a mountain, so that the one who is infinite may be surely but within limits encompassed by created nature."[17]

These ancient Christians were saying that because God became flesh and lived among normal humans, he affirmed and redeemed the created order and legitimized the place of image, art, and matter in our relationship with him. This is an incredibly liberating message for those who possess an artistic bent, who love beauty, and who have felt their souls being starved by centuries of scientism and the rationalism of the Enlightenment.

A vital relationship with God includes *both* divinity and humanity because Jesus claimed to be fully God and fully human (that'll give you a brain cramp). As God, he was able to perform miracles, teach with superhuman authority, and live above the stain of sin. As a man, he felt what we feel. He touched what we touch. He ate, drank, slept, cried, and laughed just like we do. The fact that God entered humanity affirms his continuing presence with and pleasure in the material world. At the same time, God calls humanity to rise up and be united with him in the heavens.

More and more, I'm understanding the significance of God's incarnation, made a reality when Jesus was born two thousand years ago. It helps me root my life in this world, although I never forget I'm here only temporarily and will ultimately become a citizen of another country—heaven. It encourages me to engage this world positively, pointing out glimmers of God to anyone who will look. It inspires me to enjoy art and science because both reveal the presence of God. It teaches me to be earthy as I strive at the same time to be spiritual.

Your Turn to Talk

Where are you in all of this? Are you able to see God in truth, beauty, and goodness? Are those terms even meaningful to you? Have you typically viewed God as a stingy curmudgeon opposed to just about everything? How do you react to the idea that God is mostly in favor of stuff? How could the idea of God's incarnation change the way you view life? Talk about it in your journal.

chapter six

GOD LIKES TRUTH

Embracing the Absolute

When anyone says, "This is true," are you immediately suspicious? I am. E-rumors have ruined my trust in the common claim to truth.

We've all had our in-boxes jammed with messages like this one:

Subject: This could save your life…this is true!!!

I am forwarding this e-mail about something really scary I heard about today.

On an average day, you are out and decide you are thirsty. You notice a pop machine. You go over & drop in some money. After collecting your beverage, you reach in the little compartment to collect your 50 cents change. Upon reaching in, you feel a sharp prick on the finger. You bend down and look inside to see what pricked you. What you see is a small needle with a note beside it: "YOU NOW HAVE THE HIV VIRUS."

THIS IS NOW HAPPENING IN AMERICA!!

Please pass this warning on to people you care about.

THE ABOVE SCENARIO HAPPENED TO SOMEONE

I KNOW!!! Police suspect that this is the work of a particular cult on the West Coast. The prime targets are major cities, but there's no saying that it couldn't occur in smaller towns.

Somehow someone inserts a syringe or a needle/pin that has been infected with the HIV virus into a vending machine compartment. Beside it they leave a note. TAKING A PEEK INTO ANY COMPARTMENT OF ANY PUBLIC MACHINE (PAY PHONE, VENDING MACHINE) BEFORE STICKING YOUR HAND IN THERE COULD SAVE YOUR LIFE. Be on the lookout for a note or a needle. In order for someone to read the note or get pricked by the needle, they must be in a place where, if they checked first, anyone could see it.

Don't let yourself become a victim & Please PASS on!

There are people who specialize in creating e-rumors such as this one. We all know they're almost all a farce, but people continue to forward them to everyone on their contact list. If you're like me, when you see an e-mail message that says, "FW/FW/FW/FW…This is really true," you just hit Delete and move on.[1]

At the opposite extreme, many people are so skeptical they discredit the possibility that there could be such a thing as absolute truth. They feel that what's true for me may not necessarily be true for you, and there is no truth that is universally true in all cultures at all times for all people. There is subjective truth, determined by each person's experience, but there is no objective truth that applies across the board.

In the book *The Death of Truth,* Jim Leffel has this to say regarding the popular understanding of truth:

In a recent series of more than twenty interviews conducted at random at a large university, people were asked if there was such a thing as absolute truth…. All but one respondent answered along these lines:

"Truth is whatever you believe."

"There is no absolute truth."

"If there were such a thing as absolute truth, how could we know what it is?"

"People who believe in absolute truth are dangerous."[2]

People are tired of the ideological rigidity that has ruled the world for so long. They're ready for a world that allows for more diversity, freedom, and unique expression.

I see their point. In Nazi Germany too many soldiers and citizens just went along with the dictates of National Socialism, even though it was clearly racist, imperialistic, and murderous. Six million Jews died as a result. In the United States too many citizens failed to challenge a number of social "truths"—including slavery, forcing Native Americans onto reservations, and denying voting rights to women. We could point as well to Jim Crow laws in the American South, segregated public schools nationwide, corporations increasing their profit margins by polluting the environment, nuclear proliferation, and so on.

At various points in our country's history, all of the above were "true" in the sense that they had the support of law, and a majority of the population accepted the "truth" rather than challenging it. Some of these matters have been rectified, but not all of them. So it's easy to understand why people conclude that truth is evasive and changeable, evolving over time to suit current social needs or to address particular cultural conflicts.

While I understand the rationale that holds in question the existence of absolute truth, I do believe there is a body of truth that is true for everyone in every culture for all time. But I'll be the first to acknowledge the arrogance and paranoia of a lot of people who stridently advance the absolute-truth view. A lot of the books I read by Christians argue for a return to absolutism as a needed corrective to the loss of public support for objective truth. But what happens is that people tend to fight over the idea and definition of truth while losing sight of the God who loves truth. If there is no "prime mover," as some philosophers have depicted a Higher Being, would we even be talking about such a thing as truth that applies to all people in all instances?

This may seem like splitting hairs, but until you come to see that God is a God of truth, the discussion of truth just runs in circles. So let's talk about truth from a different perspective: God likes truth, and that's why everything he has made is filled with it.

WHY SO BIG? WHY SO MUCH?

It's interesting to consider that God created the universe with truth already in place. The entire universe, as vast as it is, is held together by a massive set of truths that, if violated, would cause disaster. For example, if the earth were any closer to or farther from the sun, we'd all die. If the moon were any closer to or farther from the earth, our oceans would flood the land. Think of how many truths exist just to hold together the universe. They seem endless.

The size and magnitude of the universe is beyond comprehension. Imagine I have a long sheet of paper that stretches all the way across the room, out the door, outside the building, and continues until you can't see it anymore. Now imagine that I take a pin and poke a tiny hole in the paper. The pinhole is the earth, a speck that represents all the cities, mountains, land masses, and oceans of our planet.

About five-eighths of an inch from the first pinhole, I make another pinhole. That's the moon. Now imagine that nineteen feet away, I draw a two-inch circle to represent the sun. Six hundred feet away, the length of two football fields, we come to Neptune.

After leaving the solar system and our pinhole planets, we would have to travel along one thousand miles of paper to reach the nearest star. That's roughly the distance between Chicago and Denver.

I'm no scientist, but I've been told space is so vast that distances are measured by the distance light travels in a year. Light travels at more than 186,000 miles per second. That's so fast that if a bullet were shot at that speed and circled the earth, it would hit you seven times before you fell to the ground, even if it only took you one second to fall. At the speed of light, you could travel from Los Angeles to New York in one-sixtieth of a second. You could reach the moon in less than twelve seconds; the sun in eight minutes. But even at those speeds, it would take you 4.3 light-years to reach the nearest star. And just to cross one galaxy, such as the Milky Way, it would take you 120,000 light-years. Astronomers estimate that there are more than one hundred million galaxies.

What God has made is simply staggering.

But why did he make the universe so expansive? Because God loves truth! Not only has God made the universe, he also made all the truth that holds it together. The "stuff" that's required to maintain such an incredible quantity of matter is even more staggering than the matter itself. And as far as we know, the only speck of sand in the entire universe that God has a little help maintaining is Planet Earth (and we're doing a pretty good job messing it up). God is the ultimate scientist, engineer, and astronomer, all in one. God's truth is on display in the entire universe.

Here's a report from the Bible:

God's glory is on tour in the skies,
    God-craft on exhibit across the horizon.
Madame Day holds classes every morning,
    Professor Night lectures each evening.

Their words aren't heard,
    their voices aren't recorded,

But their silence fills the earth:
>   unspoken truth is spoken everywhere.…

That's how God's Word vaults across the skies
>   from sunrise to sunset,
Melting ice, scorching deserts,
>   warming hearts to faith.[3]

THE TRUTH CONNECTION

There's a reason God has imprinted creation with so much truth. He wants us to see him behind the truth. He wants truth to point us toward knowing him in more than a distanced, impersonal, theoretical way. If our conversation about truth stops at truth itself and does not nudge us toward God, we've missed the point and purpose of truth.

Truth isn't an end in itself. Truth is meant to be a vehicle to lead us into relationship with the God of truth. This is where rationalism went wrong. In many cases the modern era made truth the ultimate pursuit. So much so that many were willing to abandon belief in God in favor of science. There was a growing notion that God and science could not coexist. And if one had to go, it would be God.

This is a problem because God says science is supposed to confirm God's existence and nature, not deny them. "For since the creation of the world God's invisible qualities—his eternal power and divine nature—have been clearly seen, being understood from what has been made, so that men are without excuse."[4]

Do you catch the meaning of that passage? Behind every truth is God. Truth leads us to God because it bears his fingerprint. No one can honestly say that he or she didn't know there is a God or what he is like. His existence and nature are "clearly seen" through physical matter—the universe he created. Through the truth God created. God and science are not enemies!

GOD AND SCIENCE

Many people are afraid to associate God too closely with science, fearing that if he is examined under a microscope, he will be discovered to be a fraud. So, accordingly, people deemphasize the use of the mind when it comes to God and faith. This mentality compels some people to neglect deep thinking, to stay away from having an active intellectual life. They prefer a simple, unconsidered, uninformed faith. Even people who acknowledge belief in God and Jesus Christ are often afraid to think too deeply about him. They settle for a surface-level knowledge that neglects God's love for truth—and they miss out on the joy of allowing truth to point them to God in new ways.

Others are afraid to associate science too closely with God because they don't want to take the "mystery" out of faith. They're reacting against the rationalism of the modern era by abandoning intellect in favor of a more mystical approach to faith. The thought goes something like this: "The modern period is all about knowing about God; we want to know God himself. But God can't be figured out. He can only be experienced. If you involve the mind, logic, or reason, you will miss God."

I agree with the desire to get beyond cold objective facts in the life of faith. I want a full experience of God in my life, and I know full well that most things concerning God are a mystery. However, God's desire is that part of our experience with him take place in our minds. Knowing God intellectually through the pursuit of truth isn't everything, but it is part of how God wants to be known. Because God likes truth so much and has gone to such great lengths to display his love of truth in what he has made, I believe he wants us to like truth as well. The challenge for us is to avoid the rationalists' mistake: making truth our God. We can find a way to enjoy God through the active use of our minds—without worshiping truth.

ALL TRUTH IS GOD'S TRUTH

Truth is not limited to the topic of God, the Bible, or religion. Every field of study and interest has a body of truth that holds it together. Truth is written into just about anything you can think of.

- In computer technology, it's true that a Mac is different from a PC—and Mac users would insist that it's true that a Mac is far superior!
- In medicine, it's true that antibiotics fight infection.
- In space travel, it's true that the human body cannot survive in space without oxygen.
- In cosmetology, it's true that the same haircut does not look right on everybody.
- In chemistry, it's true that some elements are lethal if combined.
- In psychology, it's true that people perceive life differently.
- In agriculture, it's true that if crops lack moisture, they will not yield to their full potential.
- When you drive a car, it's true that if you run a red light, you may get killed or kill someone else.
- When you take a bath, it's true that if you drop a live wire into the water, you'll have the ultimate Jacuzzi experience.

Truth is anything that is rooted in objective fact. Further, this objective truth has consequences, whether you believe it or not. Some have called objective truth "natural law." These laws, for the most part, are beyond human control, and we must all abide by them. If you jump out of an airplane without a parachute, gravity will kill you. You accept that universal truth, so you're careful to pack a chute when you go skydiving.

If God made truth and likes it, then everything that's true in any discipline or field reflects, in some fashion, God's truth. I don't have to limit myself to talking about theology in order to love truth. I can talk about what's true in computer technology and still honor God. I can talk with the banking experts about the truths of finance and economics (Charlotte is a major banking center) and discover glimmers of God—especially when it involves mathematics, which bears so much of God's fingerprint. I can learn to write in a more effective (true) way and know that I am encountering God. All truth is God's truth, and the pursuit of all truth is a legitimate use of the minds God gave us.

You don't have to become a theologian to live a life of truth. Whatever field you're in, learn to discover the objective facts of your field, and pursue them with passion. Johann Sebastian Bach, the great composer, discovered how to do this. He mastered the truths of composition as much as any human being can. His field was music, and he pursued the truth of music with abandon. His love of music and the truth of music resulted in some of the most beautiful compositions known to humankind. Interestingly, he signed his musical compositions with the letters SDG. He even had those letters carved into his organ. What did SDG stand for? *Soli Deo Gloria,* a Latin phrase meaning "to God alone be glory." Bach understood something I so desperately want in my own life and in the lives of the people I know. He understood that pursuing the science and art of great music was honoring to God. He knew that the truth of his music would point millions of people toward God, because the truth of music reflects the truth of God—indeed, the nature and character of God.

Your Turn to Talk

If you love truth, you will think more deeply about all of life. So when it comes to pursuing God, don't throw away your mind. Use it to discover truth, and let truth turn your eyes toward God.

Become a reader. I realize that we live in a visual era, but the written word presents unique opportunities to pursue certain strains of thought. I highly recommend a book titled *Invitation to the Classics* by Louise Cowan and Os Guinness. This is a helpful guide through The Great Conversation from a Christian perspective.

Join a discussion group, even if it's an online group. In-person discussions are better, though. Choose a topic you don't know much about, and find someone to discuss it with. Don't let your conversations stop when you graduate from college. That's a great habit to maintain your whole life.

Truth has to be pursued, so go out and find it—wherever you can, whenever you can. Take some time to record your thoughts in your journal. Talk about how you associate God with truth. What is it about the idea of absolute and objective truth that makes you uncomfortable? How can you make pursuing truth a more important practice in your life? Are there other truth seekers with whom you could pair up?

Whatever truth you are exploring, I hope you'll let it point you toward God.

chapter
seven

GOD LIKES BEAUTY

The Most Attractive Thing About God

Beauty has captured the heart of humanity since the beginning of time. The Greeks put into their statues and representations of their gods their highest conceptions of human beauty. Into Aphrodite they poured all they knew of womanly charm. Into Apollo they invested all they knew of manly grace. And into Zeus they gathered all they knew of royal majesty and dignity. Clearly, they connected deity and beauty.

God is beautiful, and his beauty far surpasses the superficial traits the Greeks attributed to their gods. God is a spirit, and the beauty that characterizes him is moral and spiritual beauty. You can't express this beauty on canvas or in stone, but you can experience it with a worshipful and believing heart.

After seeing the movie *A Beautiful Mind,* the story of brilliant mathematician John Nash, I saw beauty in an area in which I had never seen it before: in the complexity of the human mind. When Nash discovers that the top-secret government case he's working on is just a delusion, he struggles to preserve his genius while keeping insanity at bay. The complexity of the human brain and, in fact, all of God's creation allude to an Artist with no limit to his creativity, beauty, complexity, and symmetry.

EVEN GREATER BEAUTY

It's not in the human brain or in nature, however, where I find the highest revelation of God's beauty. For that I turn to God himself. There is a passionate psalm in which the singer expresses his love for God's house. "One thing I ask of the LORD," he cries, "this is what I seek: that I may dwell in the house of the LORD all the days of my life." And why did he desire this perpetual abiding in God's house? As he explains: "To gaze upon the beauty of the LORD."[1] In the sanctuary, as nowhere else, the psalm writer experienced the pleasantness of the Lord, the delight of the character of God in all its wonder and perfection.

To the psalmist there was no vision comparable to this vision of divine beauty. Everything else, by comparison, was dust and ashes. He announced that he would remain in the house of the Lord the rest of his life so he could drink in God's beauty.

Beauty is not a small matter, reserved only for the "artist types." Beauty is a virtue that helps shape and define a good life. Beauty in our lives flows from interacting with the beauty of God.

Don't peg me as some gushy romantic. I love sports; I eat meat. But at the same time, I'm captivated by the beauty of God. Even better, I'm learning how to enjoy his beauty in my everyday life.

Sadly, when many people think of God, they don't think of beauty. They might suspect that God is big and powerful. But beautiful? That's pretty foreign to most people. That's why it's good for us to talk about beauty, because it's central to who God is and how he wants to be known.

LOOKING BEYOND AESTHETICS

We could talk about beauty in a couple of ways. One way is to talk about a "Christian" aesthetic. We could talk about how Christians should naturally enjoy art and music and other beautiful things, since God is the original Artist. We could talk about the history of aesthetics and how Christians toggled between embracing and minimizing art. Christians were the leading artists in Byzantium and Rome. Then, during the Reformation, some downplayed art and beauty. Later, fundamentalist and evangelical Christians in North America tended to separate themselves from such "worldly" pursuits as art.

We could argue that now, with a higher value on beauty and a healthier appreciation of the arts, Christians need to reclaim the practice of art in all its forms. Dozens of writers are holding such conversations—and have been for some time.[2]

But honestly, I find the Christian-aesthetic approach to talking about beauty and art a little empty. I would rather talk first about the beauty of God himself and how he shines that beauty into the souls of people. You could call this interior beauty or mystical beauty. A truly Christian view of beauty is an inside-out beauty. It begins with the beauty of God who is in heaven but who also dwells within his people. And it's his beauty in people that defines a person's relationship to beauty and aesthetics in the external world.

I believe the beauty of God will energize your life as it has mine.

THE BEAUTY OF GOD

God is the starting point for beauty.[3] All that is beautiful is a faint reflection of the beauty of God himself. What is it about God that is so attractive that it would cause millions of angels and God's followers to fall at his feet in praise and adoration?[4] I don't claim to have God's character all figured out, but let me point out where I see his beauty.

One overwhelming expression of God's beauty is his *holiness*. Holiness is the foundation of all goodness and moral character, which means there can be no beauty without holiness. The Bible is full of an awestricken sense of God's holiness. The first truth God wanted the ancient

Israelites to come to grips with was his holiness. They were told repeatedly, "The LORD your God is holy."[5] The laws God instituted and the books of history that detail the miraculous events and circumstances that fill the pages of the Old Testament were all meant to send one primary message: God is holy. He is unlike us in that he is completely pure, flawless, perfect.

God hasn't changed. He is still absolutely pure, and this quality of holiness is a dominant element in the beauty of the Lord. Two thousand years ago, God revealed himself as the Holy One in Jesus Christ. Jesus was "altogether lovely,"[6] and the main feature of his beauty was his holiness. The Bible tells us that Jesus "committed no sin, and no deceit was found in his mouth."[7]

Many people find it difficult to relate to the holiness of God, much less find it to be a thing of beauty. I understand. It's hard to relate to a God who is so perfect that not even angels are comfortable around him. But if God were not holy, he would have no beauty. In fact, he would cease to be God. His holiness, even though difficult for us to relate to, is one important quality that makes him so beautiful.

Think of the landscape of Switzerland. The most striking feature of Swiss scenery is its mighty mountain peaks. They are overwhelming, out of reach, unmanageable. But if you take the snow-capped peaks away and replace them with more "down-to-earth" hills, you'd destroy the *beauty* of Switzerland. In much the same way, we "destroy" the beauty of the Lord when we choose to overlook his holiness. If you view it from the right perspective, God's holiness is the thing that attracts us to him.

If you've considered exploring a relationship with God but are put off by the idea of absolute holiness, I hope you'll look at it from another angle. Allow yourself to see the beauty in God's purity. Let it draw you to him. Let it put the rest of creation—people included—in perspective, so that you will experience the awe that is inspired by God's holiness.

Breathe it in, the way you would if you were gazing at a breathtaking view of the Swiss Alps.

But don't stop at God's holiness.

God isn't beautiful only because he is holy. He also expresses beauty through his grace. Holiness by itself doesn't give us a complete picture of God's beauty. The concept of beauty in the Old Testament carries with it the idea of pleasantness and desirability. It's not just outward beauty; it's a splendor of character that causes us to long to be with the beautiful person. It is winsome and attractive. It's not something that commands only our admiration; God's beauty actually compels our love. It draws out of us a response of gratitude, longing, even worship. It's what made King David say, "One thing I ask of the LORD, this is what I seek: that I may dwell in the house of the LORD all the days of my life, *to gaze upon the beauty of the LORD* and to seek him in his temple."[8]

Holiness, by itself, wouldn't compel us to love God. Nobody would think of describing a Being who is perfectly holy as being pleasant or desirable. Other descriptions might come to mind, such as lofty, magnificent, or majestic—but not necessarily pleasant. God's holiness, considered alone, isn't "pleasant." It doesn't win our hearts. It awes us, and maybe it terrifies us. When a prophet named Isaiah saw God's holiness, he said, "Woe to me!… I am ruined! For I am a man of unclean lips."[9] Simon Peter, one of Jesus's original followers, had a similar experience. After seeing Jesus's authority over the sea, Peter said, "Go away from me, Lord; I am a sinful man!"[10] That's a natural response to encountering God's holiness. We feel small in the face of holiness, but we don't necessarily feel affection.

Something more than holiness is needed to create the beauty that attracts us to God. And that "something" is God's grace. The holiness of God might compel a person's reverence and awe; but the grace of God wins our hearts. The two together give us a complete picture of God's beauty.

That's what struck Jesus's first followers about his character. John said, "We have seen his glory, the glory of the One and Only, who came from the Father, full of grace and truth."[11] Jesus was full of grace, and that drew people to him. The grace of Christ—expressed in the humble, self-less, stooping love of Christ—shines through his life from start to finish. No wonder the common people of first-century Palestine loved to hear him teach. No wonder the outcasts of society—the tax collectors and prostitutes and other "sinners"—hung on his words. He was full of grace.

Holiness by itself can easily appear too hard and frightening. But when holiness is blended with grace, then people's hearts are won.

LOVE AND RIGHTEOUSNESS

The compelling, attractive combination we find in God is love joined with righteousness. God is more than infinite holiness; he is also endless love. He is more than the pure God who can't tolerate sin; he is the loving God who gave his Son to die to save those who sin—which includes all of us.

The combination of love and holiness is what makes God so beautiful, and so pleasant. In God, grace and truth join together. It's this heart-stirring combination of holiness and grace that makes God beautiful to me. It's also the basis by which I have come to evaluate beauty in the world. I look for glimmers of God's complete "otherness" (his perfect holiness) and his compassion (his self-giving grace) everywhere I go. And when I see them, whether in art, music, or film, I say, "That's beautiful!"

As amazing as all of this is, God's beauty does not reside solely with him in heaven. God's beauty can become our possession. One of the psalm writers prayed, "Let the beauty of the LORD our God be upon us."[12] This ancient poet was praying that the divine beauty and glory of God might become the possession of all God's people. This is God's beauty on earth, present in the lives of those who follow him.

Long ago a mystic prayed that God's people would be "good look-ing." He was referring to spiritual beauty, beauty of heart and soul and character. Beauty that alludes to God's holiness and grace in the everyday moments of life. Men, women, and children have a chance in ordinary life to reflect the beauty of the Lord in their spirits. When this happens, others are drawn to the beauty of God demonstrated in practical ways in the lives of those who follow him.

I've known many people who reflect the visible and unmistakable beauty of God. The Bible tells us that all who gaze upon the glory of the Lord are "transformed into his likeness with ever-increasing glory."[13] The most compelling argument for the validity of the Christian faith is a beautiful Christian life. A holy and loving character is the most potent and effective of all sermons. Whenever people see Christians with some of the beauty of the Lord upon them, they are compelled to take notice.

The Bible describes a time when members of the early church, in the spirit of love, sold their goods and contributed the money to meet one another's needs. They also did other things that demonstrated God's presence, such as keeping in touch with God through prayer and sharing meals with one another, praising God in gladness and thankfulness. The result of this way of life was that they enjoyed "the favor of all the people."[14] Every-one in Jerusalem—no matter their religious allegiance—was impressed by the vision these early Christians painted of the beauty of God.

I often hear about people who find a relationship with God, and when I ask what attracted them, they say, "It was the life of a Christian at work or at school." They saw the beauty of the Lord in someone's life, and it was pleasant.

THE COLORS OF GOD

One description of God's beauty has captured my attention more than any other. It's the apostle John's description of God in the book of Revelation.

John was a Christ-follower in Jesus's lifetime and was Jesus's closest friend. He was persecuted by the civil authorities and was eventually sent into exile to an island called Patmos.

While on Patmos, John was given a vision of things to come. That's what the book of Revelation is: John's vision of what God has planned for the future. And his vision included a visual display of heaven, God, and the angels.

John wrote down his description of God. What fascinates me is that he described what he saw in terms of beauty. Listen to what he said: "The one who sat there [on the throne] had the appearance of jasper and carnelian. A rainbow, resembling an emerald, encircled the throne."[15] John compared God's beauty to three gems—jasper, carnelian, and emerald. While he couldn't precisely describe the overwhelming beauty of God, John unashamedly used images of priceless, pure gems to express what he saw.

We know what an emerald is. It's a clear stone with a deep green color. Carnelian is a kind of quartz, and it's usually a reddish color. Jasper is also a kind of quartz. But in John's day, jasper could refer not just to quartz, but to any opaque precious stone. They were mostly red, but some were green, blue, brown, yellow, white, and even striped.

When it comes to God's beauty, John saw color. God does not have a color, but he uses color to help us understand how beautiful he is. God has filled his world with color, because somehow his own beauty is filled with color. We see in Revelation 21 that heaven has no need of sun or moon to shine upon it, for the glory of God is its light. God's beauty illumines all of heaven and fills its inhabitants with a perfect radiance.

God's beauty, as seen by John, fills all that is beautiful in our world. The greatest work of art or display of color on earth simply alludes to the splendor of God's beauty in heaven. I long to see churches filled with people who are enamored with the beauty of God himself. Art is a great way to get in touch with beauty, but don't stop at art. Let art grab you and lead you to the throne of God, from which true beauty flows like a river into the lives of God's people.

ASHES TRADED FOR BEAUTY

Let's talk about one more aspect of beauty that's often overlooked. That's the beauty of a changed life. In my work as the pastor of a large church, every week I saw hundreds of amazing miracles—miracles of lives that were touched, changed, and healed by God's power. Every week people brought into our church their brokenness, grief, guilt, trouble, addictions, destructive relationships, depression, and sin and exchanged them for God's liberating grace and strength. The change wasn't always instant. For many, it was a long process of growth. But the principle was in full force: God turns ashes into beauty.

In fact, God has promised to give his people "a crown of beauty instead of ashes."[16] In Bible times it was the custom for people to lie in ashes during times of deep mourning and difficulty. Think about that. You've got a problem in your life, so you sit down in a pile of ashes. There's nothing beautiful about ashes. But God says he will take your difficult, depressing, horrible situation and give you beauty in its place. He wants to pick you up out of life's ash heap and make something beautiful out of your life.

The Hebrew word for *ashes* is *epher,* and the Hebrew word for *beauty* is *pheer.* Move the *e* and you have a different word. And just as quickly as it takes you to move one letter, God can turn your sorrow into joy. He speaks, and the most repulsive ashes are turned into beauty.

You may feel as though your life has taken an ugly turn, that you're buried in insignificance. But sometimes things that appear ugly just need the right climate in which to grow. There is a species of century plant called the maguey. It grows for years, with big, coarse leaves as thick as two hands put together. It puts out sharp thorns, and it's one of the ugliest plants imaginable. The more it grows, the uglier it gets. But suddenly it sends up a tall, thick shaft. As this new growth matures, the maguey decks its spreading head with thousands of flowers and becomes an incredibly beautiful plant.

The possibility of all that fragrant beauty was always present in the detestable ugliness of the plant. Just as the fragrant beauty of your life is sometimes hidden behind pain and suffering. But painful experiences can cause beauty to come forth.

God knows we're often burned by life's experiences. But he also knows he can replace our burned-out mess with something beautiful. Whatever God's hands touch becomes beautiful.

One of the oldest books in the Bible tells the story of a righteous man named Job, who was subjected to incredible suffering and yet maintained his hold on faith. Even though Job was burdened by loss, he became beautiful when he fell down and praised God.

You've probably heard the Bible story of a young Hebrew man named Daniel, who was living in an enemy nation and was thrown into a pit with lions. In the face of almost certain death—or at least severe mauling—Daniel became beautiful when he prayed and thanked God.[17]

When Abraham, the father of all Israel, was asked to sacrifice his own son, he became beautiful when he said, "I and the boy [will] go over there. We will worship."[18]

When Hannah gave her long-awaited and much-longed-for son, Samuel, to the Lord, she became beautiful when she said, "My heart rejoices in the LORD."[19]

When the apostle Paul was thrown in prison for teaching about Jesus, he became beautiful when he said, "Rejoice in the Lord always. I will say it again: Rejoice!"[20]

Our ashes become beautiful when we allow God to heal our souls and fill us with praise and obedience. A soul healed by God's touch is more majestic than the Swiss Alps, more breathtaking than the Grand Canyon, more awe-inspiring than the Pacific Ocean.

A life changed by God is the pinnacle of God's beauty on earth.

Your Turn to Talk

Where have you seen God's beauty? Have you seen it in the lives of other people? Have you seen it in the things God has made?

Take a break and write your response to this chapter in your journal. I hope you'll begin to see God's beauty everywhere you look.

GOD LIKES GOODNESS

We Experience God Best Through His Love

I love bookstores—the smell of strong coffee, the café tables, the end-less collection of books and magazines, the jazz that's often playing, and the people who hang out in the aisles. In a bookstore, everybody seems to be looking for answers to something. Maybe they're looking for the meaning of life or just when to plant roses. People looking for answers are my kind of people.

Over the past few years, I've noticed hundreds of books that address "core values." Companies and individuals alike are trying to determine what is most valuable to them. The core-values books all follow the same line of reasoning: Establish your core values and then set the boundaries of how you operate based on your values. (I just saved you a lot of money on books.)

Values is a major theme in the political world as well. There are "tradi-tional family values" and "free-market values" and "probusiness values" and "put-America-to-work values," just to name a few. For many people, a politician's value system is as important as his economic or foreign policy.

Even churches have gotten caught up in the core-value craze. It's called the primary "purposes" of the church. A pastor in Southern California, Rick Warren, wrote a couple of wildly successful books that introduced the idea of becoming "purpose driven." There's no doubt that people want to live and work and do business according to something more grounded than personal preferences. They want to live and work and do business, and even worship, according to core values.

But I need to see and hear more than just a person's values. For my life to be transformed, I need something that reaches beyond human opinions and perspectives. I need to see the character of God.

VALUES OR VIRTUES?

I'm not knocking values. We all need them, because they keep us oriented to a fixed point and directed by something beyond mere convenience, pragmatism, or the bottom line. I have my own set of values, and I imagine you do too. I'm trying to live in light of what I value, and I encourage others to determine what they value most and live accordingly. But for me, any discussion of values eventually hits a brick wall. Values are based on any number of goals and motivations, and they vary from one individual to the next. A core value for you might not even appear on the next person's radar screen. So we need to talk about something bigger than values; we need to look at *virtues* (goodness).

When we say we value something, we're placing value on the object—investing more in our friendships or pursuing a healthier lifestyle or spending more time in nature. We value the objects we consider to have worth or importance. We even place value on certain behaviors over others. But in isolation, does any object or behavior have value? No. Its worth is based on the value we place upon it.

A virtue, on the other hand, is a quality of character that comes from within and can't be externally imposed. Its worth is inherent, not subject to the shifting whims of human preference. I want to be a person of virtue—a person whose life is grounded in an unchanging beauty of character. I want to be a "good" person in the richest sense of that overused word.

WHERE WE EXPERIENCE VIRTUE

When I look at God, I see virtue. When I see God in people, I see goodness.

God's virtue comes from deep within his character. Nothing I say or do can change his worth, because I'm not the one who assigns worth to God. His virtue emanates from within himself, making his worth and goodness internal. And because God is the source of all goodness, he likes goodness whenever and wherever he sees it.

That's why I'm learning to spot goodness in people, in culture, and in creation. Not that it's always a simple process. Goodness and evil live side by side, and it's relatively easy to point out evil. But the greater challenge is being able to point out virtue. An even greater challenge is being able to embody virtue. Can we spot glimmers of God's goodness in our broken world? Do we recognize the beauty of God's character when we see it in practice? Do we exhibit God's goodness in our everyday lives? I'm convinced that seeing God's goodness is where personal transformation occurs.

At the core of who God is, we find a magnificent, unchanging beauty of character that defines goodness in every sphere of life. If we really want to understand the basis of values and ethics, we need to get past discussing objects, no matter how noble and valuable they are, and begin a conversation on virtues. For values and ethics to make sense, they need to be rooted in virtues, the unchanging character qualities of God.

The words *ethics* and *values* often carry negative connotations. They can be thought to define what we oppose rather than what we support. But virtues are just the opposite. As we look at God's character—his goodness—we find the behaviors and attitudes that he really likes. Once again, we see a God who likes stuff—not just the material stuff of this world but also the immaterial stuff of our lives.

WHICH VIRTUES ARE VIRTUOUS?

Through the ages people have attempted to define the virtues and have often caused more confusion than clarity. The classical Greek philosophers considered the foremost virtues to be prudence, temperance, courage, and justice. Early church theologians, including Saint Gregory of Nyssa, who lived from AD 330–396, adopted these virtues—the Cardinal Virtues—and considered them to be honored equally by all people, Christian or not. The apostle Paul defined the three chief virtues as faith, hope, and love. The early church fathers called these the three Theological Virtues because they believed these virtues were not natural to humans in their fallen state but were conferred at baptism.

The Heavenly Virtues combine the four cardinal virtues: prudence, temperance, courage, and justice, with a variation of the Theological Virtues—faith, hope, and charity.

The Contrary Virtues were derived from the "Psychomachia" ("Battle for the Soul"), an epic poem written by Prudentius in AD 410. Practicing these virtues is alleged to protect one against temptation toward the Seven Deadly Sins: *humility* against pride, *kindness* against envy, *abstinence* against gluttony, *chastity* against lust, *patience* against anger, *liberality* against greed, and *diligence* against sloth.

Continuing the numerological mysticism of seven, the church assembled a list of seven good works that was included in medieval catechisms: Feed the hungry, give drink to the thirsty, give shelter to strangers, clothe the naked, visit the sick, minister to prisoners, and bury the dead.

Pretty confusing, huh? Well, let's try to simplify the virtues of God the way the apostle Paul did. He wrote, "And now these three remain: faith, hope, and love. *But the greatest of these is love.*"[1] If we had to limit our understanding of virtue to one word, the word God chooses is *love*.

Love is the greatest of all virtues and is the single one-word description of God. In fact, God is so linked to love that the Bible says, "God is love."[2]

LOVE SAYS IT ALL

When Jesus was asked about the most important commandment, he summed it up this way: " 'Love the Lord your God with all your heart and with all your soul and with all your mind and with all your strength.' The second is this: 'Love your neighbor as yourself.' There is no commandment greater than these."[3] Jesus, who was God in the flesh, confirmed that love is the primary virtue.

The apostle Paul echoed the teaching of Jesus: "Love must be sincere. Hate what is evil; cling to what is good. Be devoted to one another in brotherly love. Honor one another above yourselves."[4]

Jesus's best friend, a disciple named John, adds this: "If anyone says, 'I love God,' yet hates his brother, he is a liar. For anyone who does not love his brother, whom he has seen, cannot love God, whom he has not seen. And he has given us this command: Whoever loves God must also love his brother."[5] In other words, the true measure of whether we love God is shown in how well we love other people.

Love is the hinge that holds all other virtues together, and it is the primary character trait that defines God as "good." You can't talk about the goodness of God without talking primarily about his love. And God's love, shining into the hearts of his people, is also the defining characteristic of everyone who is in fellowship with him. Love is the number-one characteristic by which God's people should be known. Others might think of you as smart or generous or funny or loyal. Maybe people know you for your musical talent or artistic abilities. But God asks, "Do you love?"

The apostle Paul wrote:

If I speak in the tongues of men and of angels, but have not love, I am only a resounding gong or a clanging cymbal. If I have the gift of prophecy and can fathom all mysteries and all knowledge, and if I have a faith that can move mountains, but have not love, I am nothing. If I give all I possess to the poor and surrender my body to the flames, but have not love, I gain nothing.[6]

Do you see it? All abilities and experiences are empty without love being present, because love is the crown of virtue and goodness.

EXPERIENCING TRUE LOVE

God's love is not just something to talk about; it's something we can experience. God longs to show us his love. In fact, if you stop to think about it long enough, you can probably spot many ways God is already showing you his love.

What is God's love like? Here are characteristics I've discovered about God's love:

1. God loves us perfectly. If we want to experience true love, we need to receive it from God. He is the standard for all love, and he loves us with perfection. He is patient and kind. He desires the best for us. He seeks to build us up.

2. God loves us where we are. He doesn't demand that we meet certain prerequisites before he will love us. He loves us as we are. Jesus met everyone—from blue-collar workers to social outcasts to military leaders—where they were. He longed to cleanse them and make them holy, but he started the process just where he found each individual. He spoke their language and started with what they could understand. He worked to meet their unique needs.

Love doesn't demand absolute conformity. It doesn't insist that people have the same experience, the same tastes, the same background.

True love embraces people as they are. Still, as Christian author and pastor Max Lucado has said, "God loves you just the way you are, but he refuses to leave you that way."[7] God's love accepts people where they are but also calls them to "participate in the divine nature."[8] That is, we're to become more and more like God in our character.

3. God loves us for our potential. Some of us (including myself) are really good at seeing potential problems. In fact, I believe that's one of my gifts. Those around me have confirmed that I have the ability to see problems coming before they hit, and I also have the ability to find a solution before many people even know there's a problem. This is a good thing. However, I've met people who find a problem in every solution. They're not problem solvers; they're problem finders. They are harsh, cynical, and critical. A lot of people think that's how God is too. He's always looking for what's wrong. But in fact, his love proves that he's just the opposite.

When God looks at us, he sees our full potential, our emerging beauty, and his own divine image. God loves us even in our failures, because he spotlights our potential and our strengths. God loves us now based on what he knows we will become. In many ways, God is like a dedicated gardener. He gives love and attention to little seeds long before flowers or vegetables appear in the garden. He knows the potential that lies within each seed. The seed will germinate, grow, and bear fruit. Then it will create other seeds that will multiply its own life. God gives us love and attention now, even when others can't see our potential, because he knows what we will become.

4. God's love puts us first. We see God's love most clearly in his willingness to sacrifice for those he loves. God's love isn't a feeling that comes and goes depending on his mood. His love is unvarying and is best experienced in what he *does.* The full extent of God's love is seen in his willingness to sacrifice his own Son on our behalf. Jesus said, "This is the very best way to love. Put your life on the line for your friends."[9]

That's how God demonstrated his love for us: by putting his life on the line for us. God's love gives generously and sacrifices to the extreme. There is no more graphic picture of this than Jesus's battered body hanging on a bloody cross of crucifixion. Far more than a scene of unjust execution, the cross of Jesus was God's ultimate demonstration of his goodness. It was his display of perfect love. It is the enduring standard of love, even in our lives. Can you imagine what the world would look like if everyone put others ahead of their own selfish interests? That's what God's love looks like.

If you've had bad experiences with imperfect human love, I encourage you to experience the perfect love of God. Even if you've experienced the most positive aspects of human love—and I hope you've had many such experiences—I still encourage you to receive God's love. God's perfect love is available to everyone who seeks it.

Your Turn to Talk

We've reached the end of another section. Take some time to reflect on the things that God likes, such as truth, beauty, goodness (virtue), and the enjoyment of life. Record your thoughts in your journal.

part three

A CLEARER LOOK
AT GOD

*The Mosaic That Reveals
the Almighty*

chapter nine

GOD'S MOST DETAILED PORTRAIT

The Divine Canvasses and What They Show Us

Christians often refer to God as Father or heavenly Father. While this image appears throughout the Gospels in the New Testament, it's an unattractive image in the minds of many people today. For many, "father" is a person who is distant but demanding—or emotionally absent, missing completely, or possibly abusive. All children long to know their father's heart, but many fathers practice the art of silence. They keep their identity, emotions, and love hidden. If this describes your father, my heart aches for you.

It makes sense that people tend to transfer their feelings about their earthly father to their perceptions of God. Many who have had bad experiences with their fathers assume that God will ignore them, neglect them, reject them, or simply leave them alone. We feel alone already, so why multiply the loneliness by pursuing a relationship with God?

The absent-dad epidemic is growing, making belief in a knowable God a tough thing for many people. Or if they do believe in God, they struggle with the idea of knowing him up close or ever being able to interact with him. Maybe this describes you. If so, I don't blame you for struggling. I know it's difficult to think beyond your own experiences, but I hope you can find the strength to give it a try.

God isn't an absentee dad. He has taken deliberate steps to make himself known and accessible to you, to me, and to everyone else. He makes himself available to us in a great number of very creative ways. Because he desires to have a relationship with us, God has broken the silence and come out of hiding. He has done what I wish every father would do: He has shown us his heart. If you want to know God and have a relationship with him, you can! It's the same thing God wants: a relationship with you.

THE CANVAS OF CREATION

God has painted a self-portrait to show us what he's like. But his portrait is not a single canvas painting—that would be far too limiting. God's self-portrait is much more like many paintings grouped together that combine to create one incredibly detailed image. Each canvas complements the others to bring out the longings of God's heart.

The first portrait is the canvas of creation. God reveals himself to us in nature. This isn't the same thing as the Eastern belief that God is all things and is in all things. Nature is not God, and God is not nature. But nature is something God uses to show us who he is and to tell us about himself. The Bible uses poetry to speak of the canvas of creation:

> The heavens tell of the glory of God.
>   The skies display his marvelous craftsmanship.
> Day after day they continue to speak;
>   Night after night they make him known....
>
> The sun lives in the heavens
>   where God placed it.

It bursts forth like a radiant bridegroom
    after his wedding....
The sun rises at one end of the heavens
    and follows its course to the other end.
    Nothing can hide from its heat.[1]

God's creation, the entire universe, communicates an important message about God, a message we should not ignore. A Christ-follower named John Calvin said, "Wherever you cast your eyes, there is no spot in the universe where you cannot discern at least some sparks of His glory."[2]

The sun, the stars, the oceans, and the animal kingdom all paint a partial portrait of God's heart and character. And what is the message? God is glorious and stunning. He's truly awe-inspiring! When God wanted us to know about his power, his beauty, and his creativity, he created the universe and everything in it. The created order reflects the beauty and artfulness of God.

But God is not just beautiful and artistic. He is also more powerful than we can imagine. Young boys amuse me when they obsess about their dad's strength. "My dad can beat up your dad," they say. Most dads love to wrestle with their sons or pick them up using only one arm. Boys love it when their dads show off their strength.

Dads are meant to be strong, but not just physically. Dads are meant to have strength of heart, character, and resolve. Children need strong dads who make them feel safe, secure, and loved. It's no different with God. God is a strong Father who wants us to know we're safe and secure in his arms. So he created the heavens and the earth to show us how great he really is.

God's strength has been the strength of my life. My family, my health, and my relationships have all been upheld by God's strong arm. The same power that keeps the planets from colliding into one another keeps me from colliding into confusion and chaos in my daily life. The same God who filled the oceans fills my life with a reservoir of strength that I draw from regularly. God's power isn't just something I see in the sun as it lights up the sky and heats the earth. No, God's power is something I feel day by day, something I experience when I need it most. And gradually I've been learning to rely on God's strength more than I rely on myself.

But the canvas of creation is limited; it gives us only a narrowly focused snapshot of God. It only shows us God in his role as Creator. We can know about God through nature, but we can't know God *personally* through creation. That explains why those who seek God exclusively in nature end up with a deeply impersonal and confused view of God—often jumping from one religion to another as they try to make sense of this distant, disengaged deity.

There's more to God than just his greatness, power, and artistry. Although God's strength is a great starting point for knowing him, there's another canvas that adds richness, texture, and detail to our perception of God.

What's in a Name?

Because God wants us to see his heart, he gave us more than just a painting of his power. He wanted so much to connect with us personally that he told us his name. And in doing so, he showed us that he is someone we can relate to. He's someone we can know personally, as we know our best friend. He told us that he's *present* with us, not simply aware of us from a distance.

The canvas on which God has painted this personal portrait is the canvas of the Bible. The Bible is God's vehicle for delivering a highly detailed self-revelation, providing a comprehensive picture of him that we can't get from creation. In the Bible, God shows us how he interacts with people, how we are designed to relate to him, and how we can live our lives in a way that pleases him.

Read this description of God's self-revelation:

The revelation of GOD is whole
  and pulls our lives together.
The signposts of GOD are clear
  and point out the right road.
The life-maps of GOD are right,
  showing the way to joy.
The directions of GOD are plain
  and easy on the eyes.
GOD's reputation is twenty-four-carat gold,
  with a lifetime guarantee.
The decisions of GOD are accurate
  down to the nth degree.[3]

In this passage from the Bible, God's most personal name is used six times. The Hebrew term that is translated "GOD" is *Yahweh,* which is the name God gave himself. Every other term for God that is used in the Old Testament is a title, and there are many. But Yahweh is his name. When we know someone by his title, we know *about* him, but when we know him by name, we can have a relationship with him. The canvas of creation, with all its wonder and beauty, can't tell us God's name. Only God's speaking beyond nature can move us from knowing him as our Creator to knowing him as a Person.

In the verses quoted above, the words *revelation, signposts, life-maps, directions,* and *decisions* are terms that can be used to describe the first five books of the Bible: Genesis, Exodus, Leviticus, Numbers, and Deuteronomy. But when the Bible was completed, with the addition of the other thirty-four books of the Old Testament and, later, the twenty-seven books of the New Testament, God's self-revelation was also completed. Every page of the Bible shows us his heart. By interacting with God through reading, studying, and discussing the Bible, we come to know him personally; we come to know him as a God who cares for us and who wants to be with us.

This is why Christians place such a high value on the Bible. We're not just bibliophiles who love to dig into ancient texts. We believe that the Bible puts us in touch with God's heart. Even though I've spent many years studying and teaching the Bible and have even earned a couple doctorates in applying the Bible to culture and life, I'm still excited every time I open the Bible. It's not just a book of wisdom or history or poetry or biography. It is truth that connects me personally with God.

At the church I used to lead in Charlotte, we had Bible study groups, classes, discussion groups, and chat rooms all devoted to understanding the Bible more clearly. I regularly saw people's lives being transformed as they encountered the heart of God in the Bible.

If you're searching for God and want to connect with him, the Bible is the best place to turn. If you'll look for him there, you'll find him.

A REVEALING MOSAIC

I'm not a big fan of art for art's sake. Art is meant for engagement, to move the heart and soul of the viewer. Good art should do something for us—whether it simply makes us joyful for a moment or calls up deep feelings from inside us. If art doesn't move us in some fashion, the artist hasn't done her job. I know, I know; you purists will say that art is the artist's expression and has nothing to do with the viewer. Well, then she should not have painted it for others to see; she should have just thought about it or painted it and then kept it in her apartment.

God's portrait of himself in the Bible is an active artistic expression. As God reveals himself to us, our lives are affected. The Bible is good art!

Each of the names for God's written self-revelation in Psalm 19 tells us something the Bible does for us, different ways our lives are affected by God's self-portrait. I want to show you some of these tremendous benefits.

In verse 7 of Psalm 19, the Bible is called "revelation." God's revelation is his teaching. God revealed to us how we can live in a way that pleases him. We never have to wonder how we can interact with God. The Bible shows us how to have a right relationship with God.

God's revelation is "whole," which means it doesn't lack anything. Everything we need to "pull our lives together" is contained in God's revelation.

God's "signposts," mentioned in verse 7, are his indicators of the best way to live. Have you noticed how life coaches seem to be coming out of the woodwork these days? These are people who help others make decisions and live life more strategically. I'm not sure what qualifies a person to be a life coach (seems like a pretty cushy job to me), but I've noticed they all have something in common: They tell others how to live.

People want to know how to live—not just how to survive, but how to make an impact on the world. Life is tough if you're trying to handle it alone. We need trustworthy advice and guidance to succeed. Knowing that we all need life coaching, God gave us his signposts. And the coaching God gives is "clear." That means his directions are easy to understand.

God's clear signposts point out the right road. Like the road signs along a highway, the signposts in the Bible tell us the right direction to go and what to watch out for along the way. The Bible is designed to give you reliable indicators in every area of life.

God's "life-maps," mentioned in verse 8, describe the direction the Bible gives. The Bible gives us more than just signs along the way; it actually lays out the entire route for us. It tells us where we are, where we need to go, and how to get there. A lot of people feel as if they're wandering aimlessly through life—a highly frustrating feeling. God doesn't want us to be frustrated, so he gave us life-maps that show us where we need to be headed. Once we know the destination, our frustration turns into joy.

In verse 8 we also hear that God's Word provides "directions." Have you ever asked for driving directions and found them to be confusing or inaccurate? I've had this experience, and I *really* don't like it (I'm being kind). The direction the Bible gives for our lives is never inaccurate. It can always be trusted. In the midst of the constant barrage of people trying to give us directions on how to live our lives, the Bible is a tried and true guide to living successfully.

In verse 9 the Bible is referred to as God's "decisions." Have you ever been faced with a difficult decision and sought advice, only to come away even more confused about the right thing to do? Or, after making a decision, have you ever wondered if it was the right one? This is another area of life in which the Bible is a tremendous help. Many of the most important decisions we need to make are addressed in the Bible. I am not saying the Bible will give you a black-and-white answer that tells you who to marry, where to live, or what to have for dinner. But it does give you practical principles to help your decision-making process.

For many people, hearing talk about the Bible conjures images of outdated ideals and irrelevant stories. But I've found the Bible to be just the opposite. I've experienced the truth that is found there, drawing me to God's heart and giving me clear, reliable direction in life.

Maybe you don't trust the Bible, or perhaps you find the Bible difficult to understand. I assure you that the Bible is worth the effort you'll put into it. Link up with some people who can help you understand it, and I believe you'll experience the same joy I have. I highly recommend that you read Bryan Loritts's book about the Bible, titled *God on Paper*,[4] which is part of this same Dialogue of Faith series. Most important, I hope you can see what the Bible really is—God's detailed self-portrait, which he has chosen to share with you.

Your Turn to Talk

How do you respond to the idea that God has made himself known to humanity as a whole and to each person individually? Have you struggled with seeing God as a knowable Being?

How about the Bible? Does it feel like a secret code book? Many factors have led people to distrust the Bible, and you might share their skepticism. What's more important to understand at this point is that God does make himself known to us, and he uses a variety of means to accomplish that. If you truly desire to know God, it's possible to meet him. As a Christ-follower named Francis Schaeffer said back in the seventies, "He is there and he is not silent."[5] I hope you can hear God. Take some time to jot down your thoughts in your journal.

chapter ten

THE DIVINE WAYFARER

Why It's Good That God Doesn't Stand Still

H ere's the deal with God: He's on a mission. And his mission is a mystery. It's a story filled with symbolism and shadow and spread over a long period of time. I have to admit, the story of God's journey is the most intriguing one I've ever come across. I guess that's why I've devoted most of my life to telling the story.

God's mission is a lot like what happens in Tolkien's The Lord of the Rings. It's a dangerous, risky quest with lots of unpredictable interruptions. But the center of the plot is more than entertainment. The plot of this story shows you what God is like.

I want to tell you God's story. See if it doesn't bring you closer to experiencing not only who God is but also what he's doing in the world. What follows is an attempt to tell God's mystery in the form of a screenplay summary.

ACT ONE: MEETING THE DIVINE WAYFARER

God creates humanity, a man and a woman who bear God's image.[1] Adam and Eve are created in such a way that they reflect God's likeness— not physically, but mentally, spiritually, and emotionally. God creates humans so they can have a relationship with him and with one another.

God creates Adam first and places him in a beautiful garden so he can enjoy life to the max. Every day Adam enjoys God and all that God has made. There is no fear, no sickness, no death. This is everyone's idea of the perfect life.

Adam's fellowship with God is based on a mutual, voluntary relationship.[2] God agrees to supply all of Adam's needs and ensure his happiness; Adam chooses to be in fellowship with God by obeying a single command: not to eat the fruit that grows on one of the trees of the garden—the tree of the knowledge of good and evil. God makes it clear that if Adam chooses to eat some of the fruit from that tree, death will result.[3] God creates Eve, Adam's wife, before this business with the forbidden fruit takes place. She adds greatly to Adam's happiness, and she joins Adam in enjoying an intimate relationship with God.

Through the crafty influence of Satan, God's archenemy, Adam and Eve eat the forbidden fruit and break their relationship with God. They incur the punishment God promised: death.[4] They don't die physically at that time, but they do die spiritually in that they are separated from the life of God. Their sin isn't simply that they decided to eat this particular fruit; it's that they chose to break their relationship with God and live independently of him. The couple believes Satan's lie that even if they do eat the fruit, God won't really put them to death. Instead, they believe that if they eat the forbidden fruit, they'll be like to God.[5] In their simple decision to eat this fruit, Eve and Adam malign God's character and defy his claim on their lives. These are the greatest offenses that can be made against a truthful and all-powerful God.

After Adam and Eve consume the fruit, they hide from God. The Bible says they "hid themselves from the presence of the LORD."[6] This is an act of defiance. They try to trick God and continue to try to break away from their relationship with him.

God finds them, but Adam and Eve don't own up to their disobedience. Instead, they lie and play the blame game. They try to get out of the consequences they know are coming.

So God condemns them, along with all who will come after them (the entire human race), to a cursed life and certain death.[7] From then on, the human race experiences sin, death, sweaty work, pain in childbirth, misery, and futility on earth. And it gets worse. The introduction of sin into the human race results in hunger, murder, chronic disease, tragedy, and all types of violence. Adam and Eve choose death instead of life.

ACT TWO: A NEW RELATIONSHIP

With the relationship between God and mankind now broken, God makes a new covenant to restore disobedient humanity to a relationship with him. The new covenant involves a Redeemer. This Redeemer will be known as the "second Adam." Just as the first Adam disobeyed God and broke the covenant, which affected all of humanity, the second Adam will restore the relationship and redeem humanity.[8] Instead of leaving humans to suffer and die in their condemnation, God immediately sets into action a plan to redeem them from the curse and to restore the perfect life he intended for all humanity.

In an unexpected move, God reveals the new promise first to Satan—who deceived Adam and Eve. God says, "From now on, you and the woman will be enemies, and your offspring and her offspring will be enemies. He will crush your head, and you will strike his heel."[9] This saying foreshadowed the fact that God would send his own Son into the world one day. God's Son would suffer death, but through his death, the effects of the curse would be removed.

God reaches out to humanity again in love because he wants to restore the broken relationship. He puts into motion a plan that will deliver humans from the clutches of Satan and restore them to perfect relationship with God. He initiates relationship and redemption. He doesn't wait around, hoping that humans will first get their act together before he pursues them in love. When God looks at humans in their sin, he has mercy. Far from wanting to judge them, God does everything possible to enable all people to escape the curse.

Through the Redeemer, God will re-create and restore humanity's fellowship with him, and his original purpose for humans will be realized. God's promise to crush the serpent's head through the Redeemer is the basis of the rest of God's story. The divine narrative is the progressive unfolding of just who God is and what he promised to do to redeem fallen humanity.

As God's mystery unfolds, as recorded in the pages of the Old Testament, God focuses on a particular group of people, the people who will eventually become the nation of Israel. These are the people God will use to carry his promise forward. And there is no power in the universe that can prevent God from making good on his promise.

Act Three: The Ultimate Rebellion

Eventually the world becomes populated, and the entire human population, with the exception of a handful of obedient followers of God, turns against God and becomes consumed with hatred and violence. God decides to destroy the human race because of its hatred for him and for one another. He sends a flood that annihilates every living being on the earth, other than one family of humans and the pairs of animals they take with them on a large boat—the ark. Noah, his family, and the animals on board are spared.

Noah represents the faithfulness God is looking for. God restarts the human race through Noah and his three sons—Shem, Ham, and Japheth.

As the earth is populated once again, God's mission focuses on the descendants of Shem, one of Noah's sons. God renews his covenant with one of Shem's descendants, a man named Abraham.[10] He promises Abraham (initially named Abram) that he and his wife, Sarai, will have a son, even though they both are way too old to have children. Plus, Sarai has always been infertile. But that's part of God's mystery.

God promises Abraham that through his future son, Abraham's descendants will eventually be as numerous as the stars. It becomes apparent that the promised Redeemer will be a descendant of Abraham. God's mystery now focuses on one group of people: Abraham's descendants, who become the nation of Israel.

God gives Abraham and Sarai (by then renamed Sarah) a son named Isaac. Isaac has two sons named Jacob and Esau. Jacob has twelve sons, and God chooses the son named Judah over the other eleven brothers.[11] The course of God's mission now focuses on the people who will descend from the line of Judah. From out of this tribe, God will make known a Redeemer who will bring about God's promise to restore his relationship with humankind.

Among all of Judah's descendants, one will eventually become the archetype of the Redeemer. A shepherd-turned-king will foreshadow the nature of God's Promised One: regal in representing almighty God, but humble and nurturing like a lowly shepherd. The descendant of Judah who first symbolizes these traits of the promised Redeemer is David, Israel's greatest king. God will renew his promise once again to David and will propel the mission forward.[12]

Through the rise and fall of generations, God reminds humanity that he will fulfill his promise to send a Redeemer. History becomes the theater in which God carries out his mission.

ACT FOUR: THE SLAUGHTERED SACRIFICE

Long before the Redeemer arrives, God institutes a system of sacrifice. The sacrificial system is a way for the people to recognize their disobedience and rebellion and to acknowledge God's holiness and power. God shows that the only way he can forgive sin is by the shedding of blood. A life must be sacrificed. The high priest of the Jewish people enters the innermost part of the temple once a year and offers an animal sacrifice for the people. The blood sacrifice that is offered on the Day of Atonement temporarily removes the people's guilt.

However, because God is holy, even one sin is an infinite offense against an infinitely holy God, and as such, it deserves an infinite degree of punishment. So the annual sacrifice for the sins of the people proves inadequate to restore the broken relationship between God and humans. The only way sin can be permanently forgiven is if the sacrifice is of divine worth. God settles temporarily for the blood of animals, but this blood really serves only as a foreshadowing of the blood of the Redeemer, which will be the final, perfect sacrifice offered for the sins of humanity. By requiring blood for the payment of sins, God shows humankind just how holy he is.

The death of God's promised Redeemer will perfect what the system of temple sacrifice began. Finally, communion between God and humans will be restored. Meanwhile, God's mission continues to advance on earth.

ACT FIVE: THE PRESENCE

God continues to desire intimate fellowship with humans—relationships based on mutual love. The work of the Redeemer will restore humans to the immediate presence of God, the same relationship that was lost in the first act of the play, when Adam and Eve ate the fruit in the Garden of Eden. Humanity is now moving toward a fixed point: the reuniting of God with his redeemed people, with the Redeemer as the focal point.[13]

God foreshadows this renewed relationship on the stage of history. Along the way he gives humanity hints at what this restored relationship will be like. God's people begin to encounter God, learning what it will be like to have personal fellowship with him again. They discover what God is like through encounters with his power, glory, and love. The presence of God is experienced in pieces, not all at once. At first, God simply "visits" certain people. These visits are brief, temporary, and limited.[14]

Then God decides to visit humankind more frequently. He makes his presence known to many but still remains inaccessible, selective, and symbolic. He takes the form of a pillar of cloud and fire and leads the Israelites through the desert after freeing them from slavery in Egypt. He then establishes a dwelling place in a portable compartment called the ark of the covenant and, later, in a giant tent called the tabernacle. During King Solomon's time, God's presence is located in a beautiful temple built in Jerusalem. Here people come to worship God and experience his presence.

God then chooses to speak to his people once again in a clear, direct, and meaningful way, but his words are mediated through spokespeople known as prophets. These men and women hear from God and then speak his words to his chosen people.[15]

The ultimate movement of God toward humanity is still in the future. When the Redeemer arrives, God will no longer reside in the temple in Jerusalem. His presence will be available to everyone who chooses to trust the Redeemer to repair the breach in the broken relationship.

ACT SIX: THE REDEEMER REVEALED

Finally, the Redeemer is revealed—and he's not just a man. He is God himself. God leaves heaven to take on human form and is born as a baby. He is raised in a normal family, grows up like any Jewish boy of his era, and works in a trade.

But he is also different. This God-Man is the promised Redeemer, the offspring of Eve who God said would crush the serpent's head. The promised Redeemer is God himself, who comes to redeem humanity, just as he promised he would back in the Garden of Eden.

When the Redeemer comes to earth to die for the sins of humankind, it is God coming in the flesh to fulfill his own promise. He takes the punishment for sin that is intended for humanity and makes spiritual freedom and salvation available to any person who chooses to believe in him. This God-Man is Jesus Christ—born in Bethlehem, raised in Nazareth, crucified and resurrected in Jerusalem. Now God is visible, tangible, and identifiable.

Through the death of Jesus, God fulfills his own promise to deal a deathblow to Satan. Jesus's death pays the penalty for the sins of humanity and reverses the curse for all who will believe in him by faith. Jesus is raised from the dead, conquering death. But Jesus's presence among humans is temporary. After his resurrection, he returns to heaven where he waits for God the Father to culminate for all time the mission he has been advancing.

ACT SEVEN: THE RE-CREATION

The ultimate restoration won't come until God re-creates heaven and earth and allows humankind to dwell in his presence forever.[16] Satan and all of God's enemies will be cast into a lake of eternal fire, thus being ultimately "crushed."

Your Turn to Talk

Some story, huh? The greatest part is that it really happened. I hope that reading this quick summary of God's story has changed the way you see him. I hope you'll forever see him as the Divine Wayfarer who journeyed through history to deliver his promise of redemption. And think about this: His promise was made not just to humanity as a race; it was made to you personally. After giving this some thought, write down what you're thinking in your journal.

chapter eleven

GOD AND HARLEYS

Start Listening for the Rumble of God

A lot of people have trouble talking about God's existence without relying on scientific arguments, rational theories, or theological systems (insert yawn here). The modern period, marked by thinkers such as René Descartes and Wolfhart Pannenberg, attempted to ground all thinking in methodical doubt and to accept nothing as true unless they could deduce it from logic and science.

A lot of churches continue to set God in the context of rational, scientific, or theological systems. They've lost the sense of mystery and intrigue that was assumed among Jesus's pre-Enlightenment followers. When we reduce God to a set of rational "truth claims," I believe we miss the essence of what God is all about.

I'm not saying that the solution to soulless rationalism is to throw out all technical understanding and scientific inquiry. I've noticed a huge overreaction in postmodern philosophy to the fields of science and rational understanding. I suspect that when the dust settles and culture evolves into the next era, we'll come out with a better balance of science and spiritual mystery. These two do not need to be mutually exclusive. If we reduce God to only being "rational" or only being "mysterious," we'll miss the joy of knowing him in his fullness.

Every field has its technical framework, but rarely does the essence of a topic lie in the technical background; it lies in *experience*. Take my Harley as an example. There's an entire engineering process guided by PhD types who designed the inner workings of my motorcycle. If most of us were to listen to these brainiacs describe the engineering basis for a Harley, we'd be terminally bored.

But when I start the motor and hear, feel, and experience that incredible rumble, I'm hooked—okay, maybe even addicted. Stacks of detailed technical specifications for a Harley can't deliver the visceral experience of riding one.

It's the same with God. The real joy isn't so much knowing all the intricate facts about him; it's experiencing his power—his rumble—in everyday life.

Back to the Harley: In my love for the Harley mystique, I can't completely dismiss the importance of the specs that make any Harley experience possible. If the specs weren't there, I wouldn't have the experience. A good connoisseur appreciates both the technical aspects and the experiential aspects of the thing he or she is enjoying. Being a connoisseur of God involves knowing some things about him, which leads to a deeper and more meaningful experience of him.

So, want to know how God can make our life rumble with his power? Here's a blueprint of his technical specifications.

DIVINE SPECS

When it comes to a blueprint of God, it's much easier to talk about what he is not than to say what he is. This method of describing God is known as *apophatic theology*. The name comes from the Greek word *apophasis*, which means "denial." It's a method of talking about God that is used in the Eastern Orthodox Church, and although it has its potential weaknesses, I like it because it affirms that God is above human reason.

John of Damascus (AD 655–749), an ancient Eastern Orthodox Christ-follower, said, "It is plain, then, that there is a God. But what he is in his essence and nature is absolutely incomprehensible and unknowable.... All that is comprehensible about him is incomprehensibility."[1] I like that. God is there. He is knowable. But he's big enough that I can never totally figure him out. When it comes to God, there's both logic and mystery, mind and heart, understanding and experience.

Let's try an experiment. Let's use the apophatic approach to talk about God's blueprints, known among Christians as God's attributes. I want to describe God's blueprints by pointing out all the things that don't limit him. God has no limits, which makes him so unlike us.

To begin this process, think about the things that limit humans:

We're limited by space. Humans can only be in one place at one time. No matter how good we are at multitasking or how advanced our PDA is, we can never be in two places at one time.

We're limited in our knowledge. Even with more information available to us than ever before, we still will never know even a fraction of what can be known. All the advances we've made during the modern era have not even come close to tapping all the information that can be known. If the scientific age has proven anything, it's how much we really do *not* know.

We're limited by resources. We never seem to have enough money, time, or ability. Then when we do get more, we realize that we need even more. Accumulating resources is a never-ending cycle that has driven many people to addiction, isolation, and emotional illness.

However, in the same areas in which we're limited, God is unlimited. When we run out, God is just getting started. When we come up short, God stands tall. And it's in these areas of nonlimitation where we see God's technical makeup. Let me point out some of God's specs, or what theologians refer to as his attributes.

Spec No. 1: God does not have a beginning. This is called the eternality of God. God is eternal, without a beginning or an end. The Bible says, "Before the mountains were born or you brought forth the earth and the world, from everlasting to everlasting you are God."[2]

It's nearly impossible for us to conceive of someone not having a beginning. But God always was and always will be. This is reassuring to us because it tells us that since God never had a beginning, he will also never have an end. He is the one thing in life that can never be taken away from us.

Spec No. 2: God does not have the need to change. This is what is called God's immutability. The essence of God's character is always the same. He does not change over time or with shifting circumstances, the way people do. In the New Testament, the Bible says, "Jesus Christ is the same yesterday and today and forever."[3] We never have to wonder what God will be like tomorrow or a thousand years from now. Who God is today he will be forever. If you can trust God today, you'll be able to trust him forever.

Spec No. 3: God is not confined by space. This is called God's omnipresence. God is everywhere simultaneously. The Bible says,

Where can I go from your Spirit?
    Where can I flee from your presence?
If I go up to the heavens, you are there;
    if I make my bed in the depths, you are there.
If I rise on the wings of the dawn,
    if I settle on the far side of the sea,
even there your hand will guide me,
    your right hand will hold me fast.[4]

There's nowhere you can go that God is not there. That means you can't be lost from God; you can't be alone. No matter how lonely you feel for companionship, God is always there.

Spec No. 4: God is not restricted by a lack of knowledge. This is called God's omniscience. God knows everything. The psalm writer proclaims,

> O LORD, you have searched me
>> and you know me.
> You know when I sit and when I rise;
>> you perceive my thoughts from afar.
> You discern my going out and my lying down;
>> you are familiar with all my ways.
> Before a word is on my tongue
>> you know it completely, O LORD.[5]

God knows about what has happened in the past, what's happening now, and what will happen in the future. You'll never face a crisis in life that baffles God. You can never meet anyone who knows more than God. And there is no circumstance in life that calls for more knowledge and wisdom than God possesses.

Spec No. 5: God is not limited by weakness. This is called God's omnipotence. God is all-powerful. One of the oldest books in the Bible states, "I know that you can do all things; no plan of yours can be thwarted."[6] Nothing has more ability than God. No person, place, or thing can restrain him from accomplishing exactly what he wants. God was able to create all there is from nothing and even now holds all things together by the strength of his hand. He demonstrated his power once and for all when he raised Jesus Christ from the dead. When we are weak, God is strong. When we are unable, God is able. When there seems to be no way, God can make a way.

These are the basic specs that cause God to rumble in our lives. The best part of God's attributes is that they can be experienced in your life. When you enter a relationship with God, these aspects of his character will make their way into your everyday life. You'll start seeing them at work within you and around you. They will become your strength, because God himself will live within you.

Your Turn to Talk

Pretty unbelievable stuff, isn't it? Again, I'm not pretending to have God completely figured out. I've simply observed what he says about himself, I've felt the rumble of his character in my life, and I've seen him rumble in the lives of many other people.

Have you ever sensed the presence of something that went beyond human ability or knowledge? Did you ever stop to think it could be God? I believe that God is with you even as you're reading these words. If you're willing to seek him, you'll find him, and you'll find that he's more than you could ever imagine.

Take some time to reflect on God's character, and jot down some of your reflections. I find that the more we reflect on the character of God, the more desirable he becomes to us. I hope you'll experience his wonder today.

WHAT IF GOD REALLY *DOES* EXIST?

Confronting Life's Weightiest Question

Despite the fact that we live in the postmodern era, when science and reason are less credible than mystery and experience, I continue to encounter people who need official proof that God exists. By proof, they mean evidence, hard facts, logical reasoning. I understand the need for evidence, and I believe that such evidence exists for any person who truly wants to find God. Christians have used various forms of evidence to "prove" the existence of God for centuries. Later in this chapter I'll share those proofs with you, not to bully you into belief, but simply to ask you to consider them in your quest for God.

But first I'd like to discuss God's existence from a completely different angle. I'd like you to consider the personal implications of the question "What if God *does* exist?" Most people who argue about God's existence are wrangling over cold, remote facts. They reduce the discussion to the banal level of a math equation. Even if they did "prove" that God exists, who would care?

The way I see it, if God does exist, it should matter. It should get our attention, capture our imaginations, make the hair stand up on the back of our necks. If God exists, there would be dramatic implications for my life and yours. If God exists, it would alter my view of the world and the way I live. So I prefer to begin such a discussion with a far more relevant question: If God does exist, how would it change my life (and yours)?

WHAT IF GOD EXISTS?

Following are some answers to this question that I've experienced in my own life. I know that each person may emphasize something different when answering this question. God is so big that none of us will experience him in exactly the same way. Still, you might identify with some of my answers. If we can agree that God does in fact exist, I know your life would be different.

If God Exists, There Is a Reliable Basis for Determining Right and Wrong

If you agree that God really does exist, you would have a standard of right and wrong, and you would sense a need for justice. If you agree that God exists and that you've been created in his image, you would feel an obligation to defend life and human dignity. You would protect the powerless and stand up for those who are marginalized.

If God exists, then there is a standard higher than human rules and preferences. Your belief in the existence of God would change how you make moral decisions, how you view matters of ethics, and how you make lifestyle choices. Somewhere, God would factor into your view of right and wrong, because if he exists, you are accountable to him.

The Bible puts it this way: "When people do not accept divine guidance, they run wild. But whoever obeys the law is happy."[1]

If we believe God exists, he would inform our moral compasses. I'm not suggesting that those who believe in God always live moral lives. In fact, Christian researcher George Barna has shown repeatedly that religious people don't live all that differently from their nonreligious counterparts.[2] However, belief in God at least informs us of a more objective morality. Whether people choose to follow that morality is an entirely different matter.

If God Exists, Your Pain Is Not Pointless

Since the beginning of human thought, pain has presented the greatest dilemma. Every person who suffers wonders what purpose there is in pain. If God exists, and if he's the kind of God he claims to be, then pain has a purpose. An all-powerful God is able to use even the most painful parts of life for our good.

As a pastor I officiated at many funerals of both Christians and unbelievers. I noticed that the mourners from an unbeliever's family evidenced a profound sense of hopelessness. Death didn't make sense to them; it was just pure pain. On the other hand, at the funeral of a believer, though still a time of tremendous grief, there was also an overwhelming sense of hope. Belief in God lifts the hearts of hurting people, reminding them that there is life beyond pain and the grave.

A few years ago a close friend died after a long bout with cancer. My wife and I, of course, were deeply grieved over losing her. However, she was a believer, and because of that eternal perspective, all of us understood that her death was actually a door to a much better life—a life lived in the presence of God. Because of an eternal perspective, she wanted her funeral to be a New Orleans–style celebration—complete with hats, umbrellas, and music (she was from Louisiana). Some would think that was odd, but I didn't. I knew that her belief in God gave meaning even to her most difficult pain. Her husband, also a believer, shared the same sense of hope and purpose, even while he worked through the emotions and grief of losing his wife. People who believe in God hear God calling through their pain, reminding them that there's more to life than just the hurt.

C. S. Lewis, a man who experienced tremendous personal loss and pain, had this to say:

We can rest contentedly in our sins and in our stupidities, and everyone who has watched gluttons shoveling down the most exquisite foods as if they did not know what they were eating, will admit that we can ignore even pleasure. But pain insists upon being attended to. God whispers to us in our pleasures, speaks in our consciences, but shouts in our pains. It is his megaphone to rouse a deaf world.[3]

If God Exists, Your Life Has a Purpose

If there's a God and he created us, then you and I are more than some slime that happened to ooze out of the primordial soup and then eventually and accidentally evolved into humanity. We're more than accidents just converting oxygen into carbon dioxide before we decay back into the earth. If God exists, then we're here for a reason, and our life is full of value. Our accomplishments are significant, and our worth is tremendous.

If there's a God, life is full of meaning. That realization is one of the greatest a person can ever come to. I think of the huge success of Rick Warren's book *The Purpose-Driven Life,* a *New York Times* bestseller. The book is a publishing phenomenon, which is evidence that people are yearning for meaning. Warren makes the case that God has a specific purpose for every person. He taps a deep sense that most of us share: that it takes more than success to satisfy us. We need to know that our lives are making a difference. We need to feel significant.

Significance happens only when you know why you're here. With that knowledge, you also know there's meaning behind what's going on in your life.

Warren explains that the key to a life of significance, a life of purpose, is directing your life toward what matters most. If you shine a flashlight, at best you'll be able to see only a few feet in front of you. But if you take the same light and focus it, it becomes a laser. A few kilowatts of highly focused light can burn through steel. If it's even more focused, it can burn through a diamond. Similarly, when we're focused on God's purposes for our lives, we become happier, more fulfilled, and more effective people.

So what should be the focus of our lives? How can we become lasers instead of flashlights? Warren suggests that God has designed five purposes for our lives:

1. *Worshiping:* "You were planned for God's pleasure."
2. *Connecting:* "You were formed for God's family."
3. *Growing:* "You were created to become like Christ."
4. *Serving:* "You were created to serve God."
5. *Sharing:* "You were made for a mission."[4]

As we discover how to live out God's purposes for our lives, we'll experience the real joy and adventure of living. But, of course, this purpose-driven life can only occur if God exists.

If God Exists, There's Hope for the Future

If God exists, then we can expect to meet him in the afterlife. This world isn't all there is. Death isn't the end; it's just the beginning. There's an eternity waiting for us that will make the short years on earth seem like early morning mist that quickly burns away when the sun comes up.

This view of eternity puts our lives in perspective. Wayne Cordeiro, pastor of New Life Community Church in Hawaii, helped me understand life by comparing eternity to an infinite line stretching from east to west. Cordeiro says that our average lifetime is proportionate to the width of a single scratch on that line. He describes how people get so preoccupied with preserving and satisfying the "scratch" that they ignore the rest of that endless line, which is eternity.[5] As a result, the lives we do live on the scratch are frustrating and disappointing because our perspective doesn't transcend the present temporal world.

The deep hunger of the soul can't be satisfied by the promises of the material world. The human soul hungers for more than just temporary ease or wealth or thrills. We hunger for God. We long for eternity. We're desperate to live forever. And if you believe God exists, you would have all those things, and your soul would be satisfied.

These are the most important answers I can think of in response to the question "What if God does exist?" If any of them tug at your heart, and if you resonate with even one of those answers, then perhaps God's existence is worth pursuing further. I encourage you to travel that journey with an eager heart and an open mind. I believe there is good, credible evidence concerning God's existence, but it's only worth pursuing if you genuinely desire that your life would be changed by the God you find.

Arguments for God's Existence

Belief in God rests not only on experience and faith but also on concrete evidence. Theologians have offered many evidences in defense of God's existence. But for centuries four arguments in particular have provided spiritual seekers and believers with ample evidence of God's existence: the ontological argument, the cosmological argument, the teleological argument, and the moral argument.

For many people, these arguments are just what they need to be able to rest soundly in their belief in God. For others, these arguments still lack the ring of truth and the ability to resonate with their souls. And for still others, evidence of God's existence is unnecessary because they believe in God solely by faith.

God births our faith in different ways. If you're someone who requires a more intellectual basis for belief in God, these arguments will be good fodder for reflection and, hopefully, discussion. Each of the four arguments seeks to demonstrate God's existence from a different angle. As we walk through the arguments, think about which one, if any, is the most plausible.

The ontological argument. This argument, first presented by Anselm (AD 1033–1109), attempts to demonstrate that since we can conceive of

God, he must exist. It is based on a definition of God as an all-perfect being and holds that the occurrence of such a definition of God proves his existence. In other words, since humans have a concept of an all-perfect being, such a being must exist. God is greater than any being humans can conceive of. His nonexistence is inconceivable; therefore, God must exist. This is a very simple argument, but one that has caused a lot of debate throughout the years.

The cosmological argument. The name of this argument comes from the Greek word *cosmos,* which means "world" or "universe." It's based on the fact that the universe exists. Why does matter exist instead of absolutely nothing? Either the universe was always here (as in it's eternal) or the universe came into being at some point. Few people, especially in the scientific disciplines, believe that the universe is eternal. Most affirm the big bang theory, which claims that the universe came into being several billion years ago through a massive explosion of compressed matter. It's important to recognize that most scientists agree that the universe had a definite beginning.

If the universe had a beginning, then we have two choices: It came into being by random chance or it was caused. There's no good reason to think that anything would come into existence by pure chance, so it makes the most sense to believe that the universe was caused.

If the universe was caused, then we have three more choices. First, it could have been self-caused. This doesn't make any more sense than saying the universe was uncaused. How can something that doesn't exist cause itself to exist? The second option is that it was caused by something that was caused by something that was caused by something. In other words, the origins of the universe are an infinite regress of contingent causes. Again, this doesn't really explain anything. There must be something at some time that started it all. There must have been a first cause. This leads to the third option: The universe could have been caused by an eternal, noncontingent Being. And if the universe was caused by an eternal Being, then God is that eternal and uncaused Being behind the formation of the universe.

Science and logic work together in the cosmological argument to give the same message we find in the Bible: "In the beginning God created the heavens and the earth."[6]

The teleological argument. The name of this argument comes from the Greek word *teleos,* which means "end" or "purpose." This argument points to the complexity, purpose, and design found in the universe in general and especially in various life forms. It logically deduces that where there's design, there must be a Designer.

The watchmaker analogy is often used to illustrate this argument. If you're walking in a field and you find a stone, you can assume that natural processes formed it. If you find a pocket watch, however, you can assume that an intelligent designer made it. (Even the fifteen-dollar "genuine-imitation" Rolex I picked up in Beijing would lead me to believe someone created it.) You make this assumption because the watch exhibits intelligent design. It has a spring to give it motion and gears and wheels to transmit the motion. The gears are made of brass so they won't rust, the spring is made of steel (which is flexible enough to form a useful spring), and the front cover is made of glass so you can see the watch's face. It's obvious that thought and purpose went into making the watch. Trillions of years of natural processes couldn't have created it. Its complexity, purpose, and design point to the existence and activity of a watchmaker.

The universe and life within it are much bigger and more complex than a watch, and it's highly unlikely that natural processes and chance could have produced such a complex and purposeful universe. In fact, the Bible makes the teleological argument:

> The wrath of God is being revealed from heaven against all
> the godlessness and wickedness of men who suppress the

truth by their wickedness, since what may be known about God is plain to them, because God has made it plain to them. For since the creation of the world God's invisible qualities—his eternal power and divine nature—have been clearly seen, being understood from what has been made, so that men are without excuse.[7]

God says that even people who have never heard his name should recognize that there's an Intelligent Designer at work in the world. Many recent discoveries have been made in astrophysics, microbiology, genetics, and other fields of science that strengthen the biblical argument. When DNA was discovered, for instance, everyone was amazed at the incredible amount of complex information stored inside every living cell.

Some people think the teleological argument is disproved by the theory of evolution, which replaces intelligent design with random chance. While it's *possible* that dumb luck could produce all the order we see in the universe, the question is, How *likely* is it? Which makes more sense? When people thought the universe was eternal, the odds for evolution weren't that bad. Given an infinite amount of time, chance occurrences could produce a lot. But now that almost no one believes the universe is eternal, evolution and chance don't provide a plausible explanation for the order we see in the universe. On top of that, there's still no reason to think that completely natural processes could ever create even the simplest life forms from nonliving materials.

The moral argument. This argument moves from the existence of an objective moral law to the existence of a moral lawgiver. The logic of the argument goes like this:

1. Objective moral law exists.
2. Objective moral law requires a moral lawgiver.
3. A moral lawgiver must exist.

Objective moral law means that people in all cultures and civilizations throughout history have had basically the same ideas about what is right and wrong (or good and evil). The objective part means that it's not just a social custom or an idea in our heads; it's an actual fact. Almost everyone agrees that if objective moral law exists, then there must be a supernatural explanation for it. There's nothing in biology, psychology, genetics, or anything else in nature that can explain why we would all share similar concepts about what is right and wrong. It must be a supernatural law from a supernatural lawgiver.

Again, we can find this argument in the Bible: "Since they show that the requirements of the law are written on their hearts, their consciences also bearing witness, and their thoughts now accusing, now even defending them."[8]

One of the things I often hear is that God can't be real because there is too much suffering in the world. Many people have denied God's existence because of the cruelty, injustice, and evil in the world. Ironically, they're making the claim that these things are wrong, which can only be true if there is some supernatural source of moral standards and universal definitions of good and evil. This doesn't mean God created evil; it means he created us with a choice between good and evil, based on real moral laws. And when we choose evil, we experience the natural consequences of that choice. So one of the most common reasons given for not believing in God is actually an argument that supports the moral argument that posits God's existence.

Your Turn to Talk

When you consider the question of God's existence, what comes to mind? Have you given much thought to the effect in the world and in your own life if you believe God really does exist? Are the implications for your everyday life significant enough to cause you to want to pursue the question of God's existence?

If so, which of the arguments for God's existence are most helpful to you? Are you already convinced of God's existence—or do you doubt his existence? If the arguments didn't convince you, just remember: It's normal to have questions and doubts. Take some time to write down your thoughts. I pray you'll keep investigating until you find the answers you're searching for.

chapter thirteen

PRAYING THE TRINITY

The Divine Idea We Can't Explain

What do a shamrock, an egg, water/ice/steam, a triangle, and a pretzel have in common? No, they're not ingredients to an odd Irish stew; they're objects that have been used to illustrate the Trinity.

The what?

Trinity is the word used to describe the Bible's teaching that God exists as one Being in three Persons—Father, Son, and Holy Spirit.

The Christian understanding of God is that he is Three in One. Each member of the Trinity is distinct, and yet they are one in essence, power, and deity. That just means that all three are God. And the three are really one.

Confused? Me too.

I've wrestled with how to explain the concept of the Trinity. I've heard just about every explanation and defense that has been used, but no matter how you cut it, the Trinity is a mystery! You can try to define it, but you'll come up short. So how do we process the Trinity?

I want to connect you with the Trinity through an ancient form of prayer. In the church's earliest centuries, before there was a finalized Bible, the church prayed its theology. The prayers of the church taught people the core beliefs of the Christian faith as they expressed to God what was handed down from Jesus's first followers. I believe this is a practice we need to return to, especially when it comes to difficult teachings such as the Trinity.

What follows is a condensed and adapted version of one of the most ancient forms of prayer (called a liturgy) that the Christian church possesses. It was written by John Chrysostom and is still used in the Eastern Orthodox Church. I've included only a portion of the original form and have updated the language so you can follow it more easily.

As you read, or hopefully pray, through this incredible liturgy, I hope you'll catch its emphasis on the Trinity. The triune God—Father, Son, and Holy Spirit—was central to the worshiping life of early Christians. You'll discover who Jesus is, who the Holy Spirit is, and how they relate to God the Father to make up the Holy Trinity. This form of prayer leads up to the celebration of something called the Lord's Supper—the practice Christians have of eating bread and drinking wine together in memory of Jesus's death on the cross.

Rather than try to explain the Trinity to you, I'd like to put you in touch with the *mystery* of the triune God. When you finish reading this prayer, write your thoughts in your journal. I realize this is a very different way to talk about Christian doctrine—praying theology rather than discussing it—but I believe there's wisdom in this practice.

By the way, in the early church (when this prayer was written) the individual who functioned as the priest was the leader, the deacon was the assistant, and the people comprised the entire congregation.

THE DIVINE LITURGY OF ST. JOHN CHRYSOSTOM[1]

Priest: Blessed is the kingdom of the Father and the Son and the
            Holy Spirit, now and forever and to the ages of ages.
People: Amen.
Deacon: In peace let us pray to the Lord.
People: Lord, have mercy....

Priest: Lord, our God, whose power is beyond compare and whose
glory is beyond understanding, whose mercy is boundless
and whose love for us is ineffable, look upon us and upon
this holy house in your compassion. Grant to us and to
those who pray with us your abundant mercy. For to you
belong all glory, honor, and worship to the Father and the
Son and the Holy Spirit, now and forever and to the ages
of ages.

People: Amen.

Priest: For yours is the dominion, the kingdom, the power, and the
glory of the Father and the Son and the Holy Spirit, now
and forever and to the ages of ages.

People: Amen.

Save us, O Son of God, who rose from the dead, to you
we sing: Alleluia. Glory to the Father and the Son and the
Holy Spirit, now and forever and to the ages of ages. Amen.

Only begotten Son and Word of God, although immor-
tal you humbled yourself for our salvation, taking flesh from
your mother the virgin Mary and, without change, becoming man. Christ, our God, you were crucified but conquered
death by death. You are one of the Holy Trinity, glorified
with the Father and the Holy Spirit—save us....

Priest: Blessed is he who comes in the name of the Lord. Blessed are
you on the throne of glory of your kingdom, seated upon
the cherubim, now and forever and to the ages of ages.
Amen.

Shine within our hearts, loving Master, the pure light of
your divine knowledge and open the eyes of our minds that
we may comprehend the message of your gospel. Instill in
us, also, reverence for your blessed commandments, so that
having conquered sinful desires, we may pursue a spiritual

life, thinking and doing all those things that are pleasing to
you. For you, Christ our God, are the light of our souls and
bodies, and to you we give glory together with your Father
who is without beginning and your all-holy, good, and life-
giving Spirit, now and forever and to the ages of ages. Amen.

    For you are a merciful God and love mankind, and unto
you we ascribe glory to the Father, and to the Son, and to
the Holy Spirit, now and ever, and unto the ages of ages....

People: Lord, have mercy.

Priest: For unto you are due all glory, honor, and worship, to the
Father, and to the Son and to the Holy Spirit, now and ever,
and unto the ages of ages.

People: Amen.

Priest: Again, we bow before you and pray to you, O good and
loving God. Hear our supplication: Cleanse our souls and
bodies from every defilement of flesh and spirit, and grant
that we may stand before your holy altar without blame or
condemnation. Grant also, O God, progress in life, faith,
and spiritual discernment to the faithful who pray with us.
And grant that always guarded by your power we may give
glory to you, the Father and the Son and the Holy Spirit,
now and forever and to the ages of ages.

People: Amen....

Priest: Through the mercies of your only begotten Son with whom
you are blessed, together with your all-holy, good, and life-
giving Spirit, now and forever and to the ages of ages.

People: Amen.

Priest: I love you, Lord, my strength. The Lord is my rock, and my
fortress, and my deliverer.

People: Father, Son, and Holy Spirit, Trinity one in essence and
inseparable.

The Creed

People: I believe in one God, the Father, the Almighty, Creator of heaven and earth, and of all things visible and invisible. And in one Lord, Jesus Christ, the only begotten Son of God, begotten of the Father before all ages. Light of light, true God of true God, begotten, not created, of one essence with the Father, through whom all things were made.

For us and for our salvation, he came down from heaven and was incarnate by the Holy Spirit and the virgin Mary and became man.

He was crucified for us under Pontius Pilate, and he suffered and was buried.

On the third day he rose according to the Scriptures.

He ascended into heaven and is seated at the right hand of the Father.

He will come again in glory to judge the living and the dead. His kingdom will have no end.

And in the Holy Spirit, the Lord, the Giver of Life, who proceeds from the Father, who together with the Father and the Son is worshiped and glorified, who spoke through the prophets.

In one, holy, catholic, and apostolic church.

I acknowledge one baptism for the forgiveness of sins.

I expect the resurrection of the dead.

And the life of the age to come. Amen.

Priest: It is proper and right to sing to you, bless you, praise you, thank you, and worship you in all places of your dominion; for you are God ineffable, beyond comprehension, invisible, beyond understanding, existing forever and always the same; you and your only begotten Son and your Holy Spirit. You brought us into being out of nothing, and when we fell, you raised us up again. You did not cease doing everything until you led us to heaven and granted us your kingdom to come. For all these things we thank you and your only begotten Son and your Holy Spirit; for all things that we know and do not know, for blessings seen and unseen that have been bestowed upon us....

People: Holy, holy, holy, Lord Sabaoth, heaven and earth are filled with your glory. Hosanna in the highest. Blessed is he who comes in the name of the Lord. Hosanna to God in the highest....

Deacon: Having prayed for the unity of faith and for the communion of the Holy Spirit, let us commit ourselves, and one another, and our whole life to Christ our God.

People: To you, O Lord....

Priest: By the grace, mercy, and love for us of your only begotten Son, with whom you are blessed, together with your all-holy, good, and life-giving Spirit, now and forever and to the ages of ages. Amen.

Lord Jesus Christ, our God, hear us from your holy dwelling place and from the glorious throne of your kingdom. You are enthroned on high with the Father and are also invisibly present among us. Come and sanctify us, and let your pure body and precious blood be given to us by your mighty hand and through us to all your people.

People: One is Holy, one is Lord, Jesus Christ, to the glory of God the Father. Amen....

Priest: Christ our God, you are the fulfillment of the Law and the prophets. You have fulfilled all the dispensation of the Father. Fill our hearts with joy and gladness always, now and forever and to the ages of ages. Amen....

May the blessing of the Lord and his mercy come upon you through his divine grace and love always, now and forever and to the ages of ages.

People: Amen.

Priest: Glory to you, O God, our hope, glory to you. May Christ our true God who rose from the dead as a good, loving, and merciful God, have mercy upon us and save us, through the power of the precious and life-giving cross and the protection of the honorable, bodiless powers of heaven.

People: Amen.

Priest: Lord Jesus Christ, our God, have mercy on us and save us.

People: Amen.

Priest: May the holy Trinity protect all of you. May the blessing and the mercy of the Lord be with you.

Your Turn to Talk

Did the Trinity of Father, Son, and Holy Spirit become more real to you as you prayed through this ancient liturgy? Reflect on your impressions and record your thoughts in your journal.

MEETING THE SHEPHERD-GOD

A Few Final Thoughts on Experiencing the Love of God

There is probably no portion of the Bible that reveals the heart of God more clearly than Psalm 23. If I could leave you with one image of God, it would be the image of God as your Shepherd. Nothing else does as much to evoke the tenderness and beauty of what it means to live in relationship with God.

Listen to the psalmist's description of the Shepherd-God:

The LORD is my shepherd, I shall not be in want.
   He makes me lie down in green pastures,
he leads me beside quiet waters,
   he restores my soul.
He guides me in paths of righteousness
   for his name's sake.
Even though I walk
   through the valley of the shadow of death,
I will fear no evil,
   for you are with me;

your rod and your staff,
    they comfort me.

You prepare a table before me
    in the presence of my enemies.
You anoint my head with oil;
    my cup overflows.
Surely goodness and love will follow me
    all the days of my life,
and I will dwell in the house of the LORD
    forever.[1]

As I bring our conversation to a close, I want to invite you into a relationship with God as your Shepherd. I want you to know him intimately as your personal Shepherd-God. I want you to receive the seven gifts he offers, which are mentioned in this Psalm.

UNWRAPPING THE GIFTS

Psalm 23 is like a wrapped gift. Many people look at the beautiful paper and the pretty bow but never tear it open to receive the gift under the paper. They read the words of this psalm but never notice what God is actually offering to give them. I want to help you unwrap the gifts offered in this psalm and receive them into your life.

Gift No. 1: The Gift of Relationship

"The LORD is *my* shepherd, I shall not be in want." This is personal. God wants to be *your* Shepherd. He wants you to be in relationship with him. He wants to be more than a distant figure who lives in heaven. He wants to be the God who lives within your heart.

Some people see God as just a higher power. But he's so much more than that. He's a God who wants to walk with us, spend time with us. He wants to have a relationship with us. And a relationship with God is the key to living a life of satisfaction and contentment. When we belong to the Shepherd, we have the promise that we will not lack anything, because the Lord will take care of us.

I've met many people who describe having an empty feeling inside. They sense that something is missing. This psalm tells us what is missing: a relationship with God. Our deepest wants are fulfilled only when we come to see God in personal terms and to know him in a personal relationship.

Gift No. 2: The Gift of Rest

"He makes me lie down in green pastures, he leads me beside quiet waters." The Shepherd will give us rest. In a world of unrest and turmoil, what could be more appealing than true rest—rest that comes from a deep confidence that we are safe? The only way we can rest is if we're not afraid.

As you know, a shepherd cares for his or her sheep—animals that won't lie down if they are uneasy or fearful. But a good shepherd is able to help the sheep relax so that they can lie down and rest. Maybe your life has some uneasy stuff in it. God wants to give you rest by assuring you that you're going to be okay. The Great Shepherd wants to take care of you and protect you. He wants you to live confidently and to experience the deep satisfaction of rest that he provides. If you'll let him, he will lead you to green pastures of rich nourishment and the quiet waters of serenity and peace.

Gift No. 3: The Gift of Restoration

"He restores my soul." When our souls are discouraged or depressed, only God can truly renew us. Only God can lift our hearts from despair and replace our burdens with what the Bible calls "abundant life."

He does this not by taking away our pain, but by giving us a strength that is greater than our pain. In the New Testament, when two sisters named Mary and Martha had lost their brother, Lazarus, in an unexpected death, they fell into deep despair. They said, "Lord…if you had been here, [our] brother would not have died."[2]

Have you ever felt like that? "God where were you? How could you let this happen? Don't you care?" But Jesus helped these sisters go from despair to hope by reminding them that there is more to life than just the here and now. He told them, "Your brother will rise again.… I am the resurrection and the life. He who believes in me will live, even though he dies; and whoever lives and believes in me will never die. Do you believe this?"[3]

God our Shepherd restores our souls by giving us the hope of life beyond this life. Your worst pain is only a temporary circumstance. There is an eternity waiting for you, where all our pain will be erased. By fixing your heart on this hope, you'll find a new strength that will carry you—a strength you can't find anywhere else.

The question today is the same question Jesus asked the grief-stricken sisters: "Do you believe this?" Jesus made it clear that he is the way to experience true life. He is the only bridge we can walk over to get to eternal life. Jesus lived, died, and rose again to provide the free gift of eternal life. Do you believe this? Have you received that gift?

Gift No. 4: The Gift of Refining

"He guides me in paths of righteousness for his name's sake." So many of the problems that people experience are the result of walking in paths of unrighteousness. Bad choices. Harmful patterns. Regrets. Consequences. When some people look back at their past, they can't avoid being deeply disappointed, maybe even ashamed.

Do you know what I say to people who feel that way? You need a Shepherd. You've been living without the leadership of a loving Shepherd. The Shepherd leads you down new paths, paths that bring life and blessing instead of regret. God our Shepherd teaches us to live a different kind of life—a life based on love, forgiveness, purity, integrity, mercy, and servanthood, instead of greed, selfishness, impurity, dishonesty, and revenge. You can walk this new, righteous path for a lifetime, then look back and feel no regret.

Even more, when we follow the Shepherd down the path of righteous living, even when we have very little in terms of worldly possessions or status, our lives make a difference. Other people feel our influence in a positive way.

Gift No. 5: The Gift of Refuge

"Even though I walk through the valley of the shadow of death, I will fear no evil, for you are with me; your rod and your staff, they comfort me." Because we live in a fallen world, we experience pain, loss, and death— and it's not God's fault. We find in the book of Genesis that God intended life to be different, but he allowed humans to choose freely how they wanted to live. They chose to live independently of God, and we have been bearing the consequences ever since.

But God has not abandoned us. When humanity turned against God, God could have turned against us. But instead, he promised that if we would draw near to him, he would draw near to us. When we follow the Shepherd, he gives us the gift of his unending presence. The only way to survive the pain that is dealt into our lives is to walk through the pain of life with God. The presence of the Shepherd is the only thing that can get us through the dark valleys.

Sheep know that when they're in a dark valley or in any type of danger, their shepherd will lead them to higher ground. This is what God does for his followers. He leads us to higher ground. And, ultimately, he will lead us to the place where there are no more valleys. Knowing where he's leading us helps us walk through the valleys we experience.

If you feel as though you're in a valley, with darkness and fear all around, I encourage you to reach up and take the Shepherd's hand. His presence will comfort you and heal your broken heart. And he will lead you to higher ground.

Gift No. 6: The Gift of Renown

"You prepare a table before me in the presence of my enemies. You anoint my head with oil; my cup overflows." Christians often talk about "honoring" God. But it's also important to recognize that God honors his people. We know that God our Shepherd values his followers because he lavishes them with care, comfort, and provision.

God's people around the world testify that God provides for their needs and comforts them in the midst of great difficulty. Even when suffering pain or tragedy, God's people find that the Shepherd spreads a banquet table for them. He anoints their heads with oil, and fills their cups to overflowing.

God never promises to take away our difficulties; he does promise, however, to provide for us in the midst of our difficulties. We can have an abundant life even when we're hurting. That's what the Shepherd wants to do for each of us.

Gift No. 7: The Gift of Reward

"Surely goodness and love will follow me all the days of my life, and I will dwell in the house of the LORD forever." When the Lord is our Shepherd, he rewards us by causing goodness and love to follow us through life. Most people invest their best efforts in chasing the "good life." But they've got it all wrong. We can't taste goodness by chasing it. Rather, we follow the Shepherd, and goodness and mercy chase us.

Jesus described this same pattern when he said, "Seek first [God's] kingdom and his righteousness, and all these things will be given to you as well."[4] If you chase the Shepherd, you'll never be able to escape the goodness that God will lavish on you. God rewards his people day by day with expressions of his love, experiences of his grace, and extensions of his mercy.

And here's the best part: The reward of goodness and mercy never ends. The psalm writer said, "I will dwell in the house of the LORD *forever*." The "good life" that this world offers disappears the moment you attain it. But when we follow the Shepherd, goodness and mercy pursue us for all of eternity. The reward God gives to his people is a reward without end.

The seven gifts mentioned in Psalm 23 are mind-boggling. Who wouldn't want them all? Who would reject a life that is characterized by enjoying the safety, comfort, protection, and gifts of the Shepherd?

I believe God wants to give these gifts to every person. You can't earn them. You don't even deserve them. All you can do is accept them.

Maybe you're feeling the heaviness of life. Maybe you're suffering from life's hardness—the frustration, pain, loss, and brokenness that none of us can avoid. If so, then it's time to let the Shepherd carry you.

ONE FINAL THOUGHT

You and I have covered a lot of ground since chapter 1. We've talked about some pretty heavy stuff (and I've gone through a boatload of coffee). My intent has not been to push you into some type of "decision" regarding your relationship with God. Rather, I've tried to invite you into a process, a journey that will continue after you close this book—a journey to seek and find God.

I have no greater desire than to see you come to know the God we've spent so much time talking about. Maybe you do desire to establish a living relationship with him. If so, I would encourage you to find some Christian people who can walk with you. But there's also nothing stopping you from reaching out to God right now.

God sent his Son, Jesus, to die for your sins. And he wants to give you the gift of eternal life—meaning you'll live forever with him in his heavenly kingdom. If you want to receive that gift, it comes through personal faith. That means you'll need to pray and confess your sin to God, tell him you accept his gift and that you receive his Son as your Savior and Lord. It also means that you'll become a Christ-follower. Whatever the cost, Jesus wants you to live your life for him. I hope you'll make that decision.

Thanks for hanging out with me and for having this conversation. I hope we can talk again sometime.

Gotta go. My Harley's calling.

PAUL'S CONVERSATION OF FAITH

W hen we dialogue about matters of faith, it's easy to think of the conversation as a debate or, even worse, as a verbal battle. If talk of faith becomes a competition—with winners and losers—then it has taken on the wrong tone.

The icon of faith conversation is not Principles of War. Instead, it is a method of conversation that first seeks to establish common ground and shared understandings. It then moves to points of departure—where biblical faith varies from other religious systems and forms of spirituality.

This was the compelling pattern established in the first century by the apostle Paul. In a conversation shared with philosophers and thinkers in ancient Athens, Paul chose the following approach to the dialogue of faith:

> Then they took him [Paul] and brought him to a meeting of the Areopagus, where they said to him, "May we know what this new teaching is that you are presenting? You are bringing some strange ideas to our ears, and we want to know what they mean." (All the Athenians and the foreigners who lived there spent their time doing nothing but talking about and listening to the latest ideas.)
>
> Paul then stood up in the meeting of the Areopagus and

said: "Men of Athens! I see that in every way you are very religious. For as I walked around and looked carefully at your objects of worship, I even found an altar with this inscription: TO AN UNKNOWN GOD. Now what you worship as something unknown I am going to proclaim to you.

"The God who made the world and everything in it is the Lord of heaven and earth and does not live in temples built by hands. And he is not served by human hands, as if he needed anything, because he himself gives all men life and breath and everything else. From one man he made every nation of men, that they should inhabit the whole earth; and he determined the times set for them and the exact places where they should live. God did this so that men would seek him and perhaps reach out for him and find him, though he is not far from each one of us. 'For in him we live and move and have our being.' As some of your own poets have said, 'We are his offspring.'

"Therefore since we are God's offspring, we should not think that the divine being is like gold or silver or stone—an image made by man's design and skill. In the past God overlooked such ignorance, but now he commands all people everywhere to repent. For he has set a day when he will judge the world with justice by the man he has appointed. He has given proof of this to all men by raising him from the dead."

When they heard about the resurrection of the dead, some of them sneered, but others said, "We want to hear you again on this subject." At that, Paul left the Council. A few men became followers of Paul and believed. Among them was Dionysius, a member of the Areopagus, also a woman named Damaris, and a number of others. (Acts 17:19-34)

When Paul began this conversation, the Athenians were in radical opposition to his faith. Not only did they not believe in Jesus, they believed in many gods. By Jewish standards they were infidels, heathen, unclean idolaters. But notice: Paul didn't launch an attack against their religion and their culture. There was no conflict; just a great conversation.

If the church had followed Paul's example throughout the ages, Christians would have been far more effective in telling the world about God. I suggest we return to this icon and utilize it as a primary image of conversing with others on matters of faith. Paul's conversation with the Athenians provides the following pattern:

1. It was relational, not confrontational. Paul was personally involved, and he granted respect and dignity to those who disagreed with him.

2. It was affirming. Paul did not criticize the Athenians' faith and culture. I do not see one insulting word in this conversation, even though it appears that some of the listeners insulted Paul when he talked about the resurrection. In contrast, Paul affirmed the fact that the Athenians were religious, and he took positive interest in their faith and culture. If you want to stop a faith conversation real quick, go ahead and demean the other person's beliefs.

3. It was contextual. Paul presented his argument according to the Athenian style. He did not force them to talk about God in a Jewish style. He stood among their objects of worship rather than sitting as a Jewish teacher would have. He talked in their language and did things their way. The best place to talk to people about God is on their turf, in their heart language, and in their style.

4. It was incarnational. By using the word *incarnational* here, I am referring to Paul's willingness to make certain accommodations for the Athenians. This is what Jesus did in his incarnation: He accommodated himself to us. He took on human flesh and nature in order to redeem humanity.

Notice whose poems Paul quoted: those of the Athenians. Notice whose culture he referred to: that of the Athenians. He was familiar with and interested in the people with whom he was talking. He built a bridge to this group through familiarity. People need to know that Christians are not just preaching at them but are familiar with their language, their beliefs, and their culture.

NOTES

Prologue

1. Friedrich Nietzsche, *The Joyful Wisdom,* trans. Thomas Common (New York: Frederick Ungar, 1960), 167-68.

2. These two metaphors are adapted from Frank Schaeffer, *Why I Became Orthodox* (Springdale, AR: Orthodox Christian Cassettes, 1994), audio-cassette. Schaeffer uses the metaphors of "God as dinosaur" and "God as nursing-home resident" in a much different context than I'm using here.

3. I borrowed the term *faith map* from Stephen Shields. His Web site *www.faithmaps.org* is an excellent guide to faith in the postmodern era.

Chapter 2

1. Culture blinds us in another way. It limits the way we relate to God—approaching him only within the confines of our own culture. For example, characterizing God in highbrow, lowbrow, middlebrow, or nobrow terms. I have borrowed the term *nobrow* from John Seabrook, a former writer for the *New Yorker*. In his book *Nobrow: The Culture of Marketing, the Marketing of Culture* (New York: Knopf, 2000), Seabrook demonstrates how the old distinctions between elite culture and low culture have eroded into the all-consuming pop culture. I've noticed that the way people view culture often relates to how they view God. So highbrow culture views God according to classical, refined taste. Low-brow culture views God according to more "earthy" values. Middlebrow views God according to middle-class values. But all such cultural views of God are inadequate because God is not imprisoned by any one cultural norm.

Chapter 3

1. The Christian church broke into two segments—East and West—in 1054. The West acknowledged the bishop of Rome as the head of the church. Today this branch is the Roman Catholic Church. The East never acknowledged the pope's authority and continues to this day as the Eastern Orthodox Church. (See Philip Schaff, *History of the Christian Church* [Peabody, MA: Hendrickson, 1996].)

2. See Edmund Doogue, *Ecumenical News International,* Report ENI-99-0408 (October 26, 1999).

3. Acts 10:43.

4. Acts 10:34-35, MSG.

5. See 2 Peter 3:9.

6. For more details on these stories, see John 8:4-11; John 4:4-26; John 4:39-42; Luke 5:27-31; 19:1-9; Luke 7:36-50; Luke 18:16; Luke 21:1-4.

7. This is found in 1 John 4:8. The Bible is one book with two parts. The Old Testament is God's story prior to Jesus's arrival on earth. The New Testament is God's story beginning with the life of Jesus and continuing with the early spread of Christianity. I encourage you to dig deeper by reading Bryan Loritts, *God on Paper: The Bible—The Wildest Story of Passion and Pursuit You'll Ever Read* (Colorado Springs: WaterBrook, 2005).

8. Paul Hill, quoted in "Abortion Doctor's Murderer Dies by Lethal Injection," Fox News/AP (September 3, 2003), www.foxnews.com/story/0,2933,96286,00.html.

9. Roman Catholics and Protestants have historically had differing views on issues such as the religious authority of the pope, the role of the clergy, the importance of church traditions, the meaning of the sacraments, how salvation is received, and how people are supposed to worship God.

10. See Exodus 20:4,23.

11. Exodus 32:27.

12. Matthew 5:45.

13. Matthew 5:47-48.

14. Matthew 5:3-10.

15. See John 1:18.

16. Psalm 97:1-2,4-6.

17. 1 Corinthians 1:18,25.

18. John 14:7,9.

19. Exodus 33:18.

20. See Romans 1:20.

21. Matthew 26:52-53.

22. John 13:14-15.

Chapter 4

1. While God has standards and rules, he never intended for us to reduce life to conformity and rule keeping. The strictest sect of Jewish religious experts in Jesus's day, the Pharisees, turned life into a series of rules—hundreds of them. And Jesus criticized them for it (see Matthew 23). God desires a love relationship with us, not a life of rule keeping

2. Ephesians 3:20.

3. Leonard Sweet, "A World at Risk," sermon delivered on November 17, 2002. To read the entire sermon, see *www.preachingplus.com.* Sweet takes this story in a totally different direction, focusing on the relationship between risk and accomplishment.

4. Hebrews 11:1, KJV.

5. These odds—1 in 344,000—equate to an annualized theoretical murder rate of 7.5 for every 100,000 people. That compares with a murder rate of 3.4 for those same Maryland and Virginia counties in 2000 (the last year for which all figures are available). See "The Logic of Irrational Fear," *The Economist* 365, no. 8295 (October 19, 2002): 29-30.

6. Statistics from the National Safety Council, cited in Mark Memmott, "Fear May Be Overwhelming, but So Are the Odds," *USA Today,* October 18, 2002.

7. You can read about this event in Joshua 2–6.

8. See Matthew 1:5.

Chapter 5

1. C. S. Lewis, *A Preface to Paradise Lost* (New York: Oxford University Press, 1961), 89.

2. According to Marilyn Ferguson, the New Age movement is the direct descendant of Gnosticism. See Marilyn Ferguson, *The Aquarian Conspiracy: Personal and Social Transformation in Our Time* (New York: St. Martin's, 1987), 120.

3. Eric Voegelin, *Science, Politics, and Gnosticism* (Chicago: Regnery Gateway, 1968), 9.

4. If you don't believe that God created the universe, continue on with me in this conversation anyway. You might see something that will cause you to stop and consider the possibility.

5. Genesis 1:31.

6. See Genesis 2:15.

7. Romans 1:20.

8. John Calvin, *Institutes of the Christian Religion,* trans. Henry Beveridge (Grand Rapids: Eerdmans, 1989), 1.14.20.

9. Charles Dickens, *Hard Times* (New York: Penguin, 1980), 11.

10. John Piper uses this statement to summarize his idea of "Christian hedonism" in almost all of his books, including *Desiring God: Meditations of a Christian Hedonist* (Sisters, OR: Multnomah, 2003) and *The Pleasures of God: Meditations on God's Delight in Being God* (Sisters, OR: Multnomah, 2000). When he refers to Christian hedonism, Piper means that God wants us to seek our own desire and happiness in God. The happier and more satisfied we are in God, the more God is glorified. Christian hedonism has roots in the writings of Blaise Pascal, Jonathan Edwards, and C. S. Lewis. This is a healthy tonic against the sour and passionless faith that has marked much of the Christian church in the modern era.

11. Blaise Pascal, *Pascal's Pensées,* trans. W. F. Trotter (New York: E. P. Dutton, 1958), 113.

12. See Mortimer Adler, *The Great Ideas: A Syntopicon of Great Books of the Western World,* 2nd. ed., 2 vols. (Chicago: Encyclopedia Britannica, 1990).

13. Sri Aurobindo, *The Life Divine,* bk. 2, chap. 25, quoted in *The Future Evolution of Man: The Divine Life on Earth* (Twin Lakes, WI: Lotus, 2002).

14. See *The Urantia Book* (Chicago: The Urantia Foundation, 1999), paper 56, sec. 10.

15. Psalm 19:1,4.

16. John of Damascus, quoted in P. Bonifatius Kotter O.S.B., *Patristische Texte und Studien,* vol. 17 (Berlin: de Gruyter, 1979), 89.1-4; 92.90-91; Alister E. McGrath, ed., *The Christian Theology Reader* (Cambridge, MA: Blackwell, 1995), 150-51.

17. Gregory Palamas, quoted in J. P. Migne, *Patrologia Graeca* (Paris, 1856–1866), 151; McGrath, *The Christian Theology Reader,* 151.

Chapter 6

1. A great Web site, *www.truthorfiction.com,* verifies the truthfulness of these kinds of rumors.

2. Jim Leffel, quoted in Dennis McCallum, ed., *The Death of Truth: Finding Your Way Through the Maze of Multiculturalism, Inclusivism, and the New Postmodern Diversity* (Minneapolis: Bethany House, 1996), 31.

3. Psalm 19:1-4,6, MSG.

4. Romans 1:20.

Chapter 7

1. Psalm 27:4.

2. If you're interested in pursuing this topic in greater depth, I'd recommend the works of Leland Ryken, Gene Edward Veith Jr., and the late

Francis Schaeffer. These thinkers are Christians who call for a Christian engagement with the arts.

3. I owe much of my thinking on God's beauty to nineteenth-century British pastor J. D. Jones. In a message titled "The Beauty of the Lord," Jones captured what I believe is at the heart of divine beauty. To my knowledge, there is no printed version of the sermon available, so in this section I have attempted to summarize in contemporary language what Jones taught his congregation about the beauty of the Lord.

4. See Revelation 4 as just one example of God's beauty eliciting dramatic praise.

5. See, for instance, Leviticus 11:44 and 1 Peter 1:16.

6. Song of Songs 5:16.

7. 1 Peter 2:22.

8. Psalm 27:4.

9. Isaiah 6:5.

10. Luke 5:8.

11. John 1:14.

12. Psalm 90:17, KJV.

13. 2 Corinthians 3:18.

14. Acts 2:47.

15. Revelation 4:3.

16. Isaiah 61:3.

17. To read about Daniel in the den of lions, see Daniel 6.

18. Genesis 22:5.

19. 1 Samuel 2:1.

20. Philippians 4:4.

Chapter 8

1. 1 Corinthians 13:13.

2. 1 John 4:8.

3. Mark 12:30.

4. Romans 12:9-10.

5. 1 John 4:20-21.

6. 1 Corinthians 13:1-3.

7. Max Lucado, *Just Like Jesus* (Nashville: W Publishing, 2003), 3.

8. 2 Peter 1:4.

9. John 15:13, MSG.

Chapter 9

1. Psalm 19:1-2,4-6, NLT.

2. John Calvin, *Institutes of the Christian Religion,* trans. Henry Beveridge (Grand Rapids: Eerdmans, 1993), I.V.1.

3. Psalm 19:7-9, MSG.

4. Bryan Loritts, *God on Paper: The Bible—The Wildest Story of Passion and Pursuit You'll Ever Read* (Colorado Springs: WaterBrook, 2005).

5. Francis A. Schaeffer, *He Is There and He Is Not Silent* (Wheaton: Tyndale, 1972).

Chapter 10

1. See Genesis 1:26.

2. See Genesis 2:15-17.

3. See Genesis 2:16-17.

4. See Genesis 3:1-13.

5. See Genesis 3:4-6.

6. Genesis 3:8, KJV.

7. See Genesis 3:14-19.

8. See Genesis 3:15,21 and Romans 5:12-21.

9. Genesis 3:15, NLT.

10. See Genesis 12:2-3.

11. See Genesis 49:8.

12. See 2 Samuel 7:8-16.

13. See Ephesians 1:10.

14. For instance, God visits Abraham (see Genesis 17:1; 18:1), Isaac (see Genesis 26:2-5), and Jacob (see Genesis 32:24-30; 35:9-13).

15. See Jeremiah 1:4-10.

16. See Revelation 21:3.

Chapter 11

1. John of Damascus, quoted in Philip Sherrard, *The Greek East and the Latin West: A Study in the Christian Tradition* (London: Oxford University Press, 1959), 32-33.

2. Psalm 90:2.

3. Hebrews 13:8.

4. Psalm 139:7-10.

5. Psalm 139:1-4.

6. Job 42:2.

Chapter 12

1. Proverbs 29:18, NLT.

2. See *www.barna.org* for details on George Barna's research in this area.

3. C. S. Lewis, *The Problem of Pain* (New York: Macmillan, 1940), 93. By the way, if you want a moving glimpse of how a believer processes pain, I recommend you rent the video *Shadowlands,* starring Anthony Hopkins and directed by Richard Attenborough (United Kingdom: Savoy Pictures, 1993). It tells the life story of C. S. Lewis and beautifully captures his struggle with the pain of losing his wife, Joy.

4. Rick Warren, *The Purpose-Driven Life: What on Earth Am I Here For?* (Grand Rapids: Zondervan, 2002).

5. See Wayne Cordeiro, *Doing Church As a Team* (Ventura, CA: Regal, 2001), 24, 25.

6. Genesis 1:1.

7. Romans 1:18-20.

8. Romans 2:15.

Chapter 13

1. John Chrysostom, adapted from Theodore Bobosh, trans., *The Divine Liturgy According to St. John Chrysostom* (Minneapolis: Light and Life, 1989). Used by permission. See also www.ocf.org/OrthodoxPage/liturgy. *The Divine Liturgy* contains the complete liturgy in English, translated from the original prayer.

Epilogue

1. Psalm 23:1-6.
2. John 11:21.
3. John 11:23,25-26.
4. Matthew 6:33.

Join the conversation about God, the Bible, and the Church

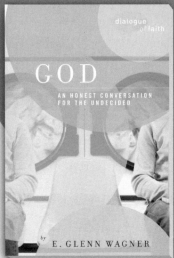

The new Dialogue of Faith series connects the timelessness of God's truth to the current questions, values, and life challenges of post-modern life.

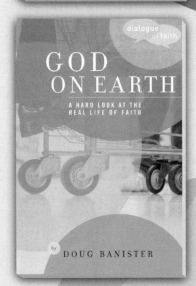

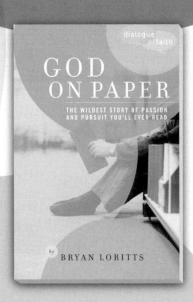